"I disappeared inside my mind in 1988 and I never came back until 2014. During this time I did what I had to do"

INDEX OF CONTENTS

PROLOGUE 5
1 MY OWN STORY 7
    1.1   WHY ME? 7
    1.2   THE DAY I SUFFERED A DEREALIZATION ATTACK 12
    1.3   MY RECOVERY 16
2 WHAT ARE THE SYMPTOMS OF DPDR DISSOCIATION? 19
    2.1   THE SENSE OF SIGHT 20
    2.2   THE SENSE OF HEARING 24
    2.3   THE SENSES OF TOUCH, SMELL AND TASTE 28
    2.4   ALTERED PERCEPTION OF TIME AND SPACE 29
    2.5   THE MEMORY 32
    2.6   NO ACCESS TO PERSONAL HISTORY AND EXISTENCIAL QUESTIONS 35
        2.7   EMOTIONS, PREFERENCES AND DECISION MAKING 36
        2.8   SOCIAL BEHAVIOUR 38
3 UNDERSTANDING OUR BRAIN A LITTLE BIT 40
    3.1   LEFT HEMISPHERE OF BRAIN 41
    3.2   RIGHT HEMISPHERE OF BRAIN 42
        3.3   SOME RELIABLE SCIENTIFIC SOURCE 45
4 WHAT IS CONSCIOUSNESS? 51
5 FREQUENT CAUSES. WHY DOES IT HAPPEN? 55
6 LIVING WITHOUT EMOTIONAL COMPONENTS 59
7 MY NATURAL METHOD TO BEAT THE DPDR DISSOCIATION 66
    7.1   INTRODUCTION TO "SANTOS BARRIOS METHOD" © 66
    7.2   BASIC PRINCIPLES OF THE METHOD 68
    7.3   THE TWENTY BASIC EXERCISES 70
        BASIC EXERCISES 1 AND 2 71
        EXERCISES TO TREAT DEREALIZATION (3, 4, 7, 8, 11, 12 y 18) 71
        EXERCISES TO TREAT DEPERSONALIZATION (5, 10, 13, 14, 16 y 20) 72
        EXERCISES TO ACQUIRE GOOD HABITS (6, 9, 15, 17 y 19) 73

EXERCISE nº1 - "Sensory walking" 76

EXERCISE nº2 - "Consciously and individual approximation to objects" 78

EXERCISE nº3 - "Let's work the time" 80

EXERCISE nº4 - "Synchronization of senses" 82

EXERCISE nº4 - "Synchronization of senses" 82

EXERCISE nº5 - "Using a bridge object" 85

EXERCISE nº6 - "Connecting every 10 minutes" 87

EXERCISE nº7 - "Active look" 90

EXERCISE nº8 - "Can anybody hear me?" 92

EXERCISE nº9 - "Visiting a shop" 94

EXERCISE nº10 - "Keep in mind others, specially parents and siblings" 97

EXERCISE Nº11 - "Getting better while driving" 99

EXERCISE nº12 - "Comparing, comparing and comparing again" 101

EXERCISE Nº13 - "The story of my life" 104

EXERCISE nº14 – The house of my childhood - "My known paths" 107

EXERCISE Nº15 - "Playing again with toys and dolls" 109

EXERCISE nº16 - "Bridge music" 111

EXERCISE nº17 - "Reading books?" 114

EXERCISE Nº18 - "Managing landscapes and open spaces" 117

EXERCISE nº19 - "Avoiding screen-based devices" 120

EXERCISE nº20 - "What should I think of others while walking on the street?" 122

    7.4   HOW IS THE RECOVERY PROCESS? 125

    7.5   WHEN WILL I KNOW THAT I AM CURED? 127

8   CONCLUSIONS 130

APPENDIX 134

TEMPLATE FOR "THE STORY OF MY LIFE" EXERCISE 135

DECALOGUE TO FOLLOW 136

DPDR AUTODIAGNOSTIC TEST 137

BLOG, VIDEOS and ASEDEP ASSOCIATION 138

PROLOGUE

Sometimes life leads us through roads very little transited. My personal experience during twenty six years living the symptoms of a, at first sight, strange dissociation called "derealization and depersonalization" changed my life and opened doors to a parallel reality for me, to the invisible community of **people passing through life without feeling they are really alive.**

The silent and misunderstood torture lived by millions of people **must come out into the open at last**. *There are people incapable of living their lives, passing through the life missing their selves, unable to enjoy their lives, into a strange and unrelated world. Many of them* **do not know to explain what is wrong with them** *and without full potential; they must be contented with leading a limited, automatic and almost emotionless life.*

Derealization?, Depersonalization?,... very few people know the meaning of these words while other terms as "anxiety" or "depression", are very well known by patients, psychologists and psychiatrists.

This dissociation, generally consequence from a **generalized anxiety** *or a* **post-traumatic stress disorder (PTSD)**, *can affect at* **different levels**. *Some people easily accustom to feel "strangeness" while others become suffering strong depersonalization and derealization symptoms requiring psychiatric care.*

The edition of this book has several objectives, firstly, helping **to spread all over the world this mental disorder named depersonalization – derealization (DPDR),** *much more common than it might appear at first sight. My approach corresponds to the understanding of this dissociation as Telecommunication Engineer, specialized on computer networks, different and complementary to the point of view of other relevant professionals as psychologists, psychiatrics and neurologists. They would be able to validate my hypothesis about the nature of this disorder.*

*Secondly, I would like to contribute as a **source of inspiration in order to design a definitive treatment against DPDR.** I expose a plausible hypothesis of the disorder nature that should be conveniently validated through clinic studies.*

*Thirdly, and the most important, **helping to the greatest number of persons to escape from this situation** describing the basis of the 'Natural Santos Barrios Method' which I set up almost accidentally during the year and a half that more or less took me to recover from DPDR.*

*This first volume is structured in eight chapters including an annex with some complementary resources. In the first chapter I describe **my own personal story**; I believe this is something important in order to identify the reasons that led me to DPDR disorder. In the second chapter I proceed to describe **the most important symptoms** of this dissociation. In the third one I explain the basic **structure of the brain needed to understand the nature** of this disorder. In the fourth I describe, in my own words, **what the consciousness** of a human being is. In the fifth chapter, there are discussed the **frequent reasons** that origin DPDR. In the sixth I narrate **how the life of a dissociated person is**, almost without feeling any emotion. In the seventh I introduce **the basis of my natural method** to fight against depersonalization and derealization. Finally, in the eighth chapter I present my **conclusions** and give a **final special message** to my readers.*

1 MY OWN STORY

1.1 WHY ME?

It was still warm on October 3rd, 1967 when I was borned in Madrid, in the bosom of a middle-class family being the youngest of three brothers. I always stood out for my academic skills and not so much for the social ones. I was a little bit shy, I didn't particularly enjoy the visits and I didn't like to have many friends, just a handful of them. We could say I used to be **introverted**; however I was a normal and happy child.

Standing on the balcony of the first house I lived

I liked **to play football** on the street, I enjoyed a lot making constructions with TENTE and EXIN building blocks (nowadays as LEGO blocks), playing parchessi with my family (my favorite color was blue), playing domino with my grandparent and I consider I had a very good and peaceful childhood. In those days, in the seventies, summers were long. Electronic devices to spend time did not exist yet. We were plenty of dull moments in contrast to the twenty-first century, when we miss them a lot.

Approximately at the age of seven or eight **my father taught me to play chess** and I quickly felt addiction for this board game. I loved it, I liked to move chess pieces and think of their possibilities on the board. It was designed for me, it meant a way to make relationships with other people while learning and growing as a chess player. I could hardly wait for playing against my father or my brother. I was really very good at it.

We were a normal family, in summer we used to go a fortnight to the beach on holiday, some weekends we went to visit my father's sister who lived on her own to a small town in Toledo. At home we used to receive visits from our relatives at Christmas, birthdays and other festivities.

Holding my parents' hands, on the "Rambla" in Alicante, 70's

We all grew up and I went to school normally. At the end of the fourth course I changed to another school where I finished my secondary schooling with good marks.

In 1979, being twelve, I began going to a chess club close to my neighborhood. In this way my chess career started. I used to study chess books, take part in tournaments and I even got several successes: champion of my club, Madrid champion at the age of thirteen, Madrid under-18 category sub champion at the age of sixteen,... chess filled my life considerably, providing me self-esteem and a world of relationships with other chess players. It was my favourite hobby and I become an outstanding chess player in Madrid, the Spanish capital.

I invested a lot of time to the practice of chess during my childhood and youth

An important event happened in summer 1981, close to the age of fourteen, **my father suffered a hemorrhagic brain stroke because of a large increase of blood** and he was very near to death. He stayed fifteen days in a intensive care unit. I thought I was going to lose my father. After many months recovering in several hospitals my father overcame it. As a consecuence the right side of his body left partially paralyzed and unable to work any more. In that way I learnt first-hand the consecuences of suffering a blood clot at the left hemisphere of the brain. Not my father didn't know me, he could recognize me, could know who I was and he felt emotions. However he wasn't able even to say my name. He had to relearn to speaking and writing with his left hand and he never was the same again.

In those days, as a teenager I became interested on girls. I began to go to discos, pubs, and dating with a girl just before the University Orientation Course (pre-university course in Spain). I started university level with a very demanding career, Telecommunication Engineering.

Photos of the summer in Cullera, Valencia in 1983

I combined my hard studies with practicing chess and my courtship. I tried to do my best, 100%, in every aspect, but **I didn't rest enough**

and relax my mind as necessary. I literally was running everywhere, firstly I tried to please my girlfriend, who was very jealous and she pretended to change my way of being, secondly to meet expectations on my higher engineering career and lastly continue playing chess at high level.

Now I know, **my mind was always busy on those three anxiety spheres since the end of 1984 till the day all of this occurred** in April, 1988, when my mind was fractured. **I didn't leave a single space for thinking about me**, my personality simply was emptied. During three years and a half I stopped thinking of me, I didn't make a summary of my life, I underestimated my own emotions, I did not assess the significant events were taking place in my life, I did things that I really didn't want to do, I was permanently concerned about the preparation and the dates of the examinations. In view of the above and taking all these considerations together it was logic that my brain was broken at some unknown spot.

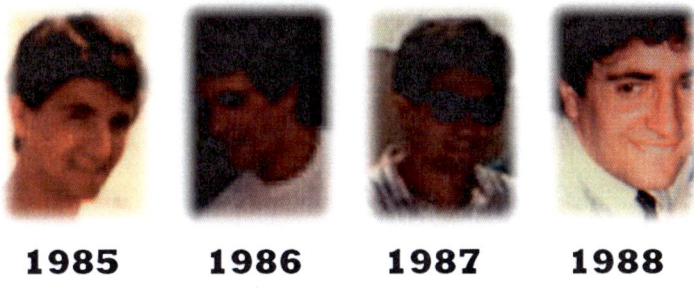

From 17 to 20, years of normalcy previous to my DPDR attack

During these years major changes were produced in my life: starting a **couple relationship** (giving up certain things, new friendships not precisely chosen by me, new places, new customs not always according to my personality,...) and beginning **a very difficult and demanding university career,** both aspects demanded much more from me that my mind could cope at these moments.

I was never aware that I was taking a risk. What could be wrong on maintaining a relationship at the same time I was studying a difficult career and continue playing chess?

1.2   THE DAY I SUFFERED A DEREALIZATION ATTACK

"Suddenly, my brain switched off. I noticed something was wrong, quite wrong. Instantaneously everything seemed far, my world turned to be strange, more gray, flatter, hearing the sounds as muffled, my body didn't seem to be completely mine and I lacked having objectives and goals in my life. I was not assured about who I was. I lost the thread in all aspects of life. I was unable to think clearly"

This way I used to perceive myself more or less in 1988, newly depersonalized

It was around noon on Monday, April 4th in 1988, I was twenty years old and I was **mounted on a tractor toward a small chapel** where a Holy Week pilgrimage will be celebrated in a village within the province of Badajoz called Campanario. A completely hostile scenario for me, **an environment contrary to my preferences, but withstood because I wanted to please my girlfriend**. In that place my story began. A happy ending story but that took more than twenty six years to be ended.

I was studying third course of Telecommunication Engineering and I already was an outstanding chess player in Madrid. I seemed to remember **experiencing the same feeling of detachment once before**, How long before? I am not sure, maybe some months or even a year before. It was an evening while I was playing a chess game in my chess club in Moratalaz neighborhood, in Madrid. Suddenly, I felt detached from the world, as in a cloud, my SELF went away,… It was the same feeling, for those who never have suffered this dissociation, as putting your head inside a diver's helmet, isolated from the world, as separated by a transparent barrier, feeling **everything cushioned**. I came back home very worried, I did not talk about it, I went to bed soon and the next morning, in a reassuring manner, I woke up ok, the detachment feeling had disappeared.

However this occasion, in April 1988, was different, when I got back home, I went to bed trusting on waking up normally next morning, thinking of everything would be ok like the last time, but not this time. Nor the next day or the next week… I would **never be ok till November 2014 when I could think clearly again.**

Twenty six years of desperation and confusion, thinking: *what the hell it's wrong with me?, why me?, this thing sooner or later will be fixed!, how long will I stay this way?, what must I do now with my life?,…* so many questions that nobody could clarify to me at that moment.

Despite of feeling **very strange and see the world like looking through a glass**, surprisingly, I kept doing certain tasks reasonably well, as playing chess almost mechanically. However, I stopped enjoying and progressing in my chess career.

Reasonably, I knew that everything I learnt throughout my life, my personal and professional experiences, everything should still be inside my brain. I didn't make any sense that my intelligence, my self, my world, had suddenly vanished. Nevertheless, everything was so confusing to me!

I wasn't suffering amnesia because making some efforts I could remember everything had occurred to me. But **my memories weren't as before**, they were diffused, vague, fragmented and emotionless.

Then the time had come to tell my family what was happening to me. My mother accompanied me to our family doctor (he was unable to understand my 'strange' symptoms), to making some clinical tests, an EEG (electroencephalogram),... EVERYTHING WAS PHYSICALLY NORMAL. I even visited a psychiatrist. As soon as I noticed he had not understood a single word of my testimony then I made the decision of not taking any pill he prescribed to me. The fact was I never came back to be the same in decades. "Santi" disappeared that April in 1988, my self was disintegrated within my own mind. How could I explain anybody what was happening to me? I stopped telling people what I felt and resigned to live with that.

From that moment on, without any excitement, confused, in a haze, mi life was based on **doing what I supposed to do in any moment**. I pretended to be normal in the eyes of the rest of persons, but inside my mind I was fully aware of this rare state of thinking. I finished the 87-88 course as I could, applying to the exams of few subjects since I could not focused on anything. It was as if my brain was unable to retain new contents.

I ended the relationship with my first girlfriend in December, 1989 because I was unable to feel nothing about her in this mental state. I kept playing chess automatically. I gave classes of chess and computer basics in a school at the center of Madrid in order to get some money and at least feel useful before my mother.

In the middle of the image, during a barbecue in 1992, pretending be normal

In 1993 I met a girl who now is my wife and the same year I also carried out military service, fortunately being depersonalized, certainly not too bad for me! In 1994 I could continue with my engineering studies regularly, not knowing really how I did and encouraged by my girlfriend Almudena who already knew I had suffered a loss of academic performance in 1988. It is thanks to her, to her insistence, I could obtain my driving license at the first opportunity in 1995 and finishing my studies in 1998.

I got a paid job in an IT (Information Technology) consultant firm in February 1998, we signed a mortgage to buy a house, we got married in 2000 and consolidated my job as a sales trainer in the most important Spanish telecommunication company, Telefónica. Then came my children, in 2004 was born Sergio and in 2007 my daughter Sofía. My life was a normal life with all I needed to be happy.

During the years I lived suffering Depersonalization and Derealization I **sometimes tried to do something to become the same person again**. I wrote a lot on loose papers, I tried to recall concepts I had learnt during my university career, especially before my DPDR stroke, but without order or harmony. **Sometimes I felt a little better reliving or talking to someone about certain aspects of my past**, but it was as lashing out in the dark. I lacked the continuity to be able to recover from something if I did not even know its name.

1.3   MY RECOVERY

It wasn't until the beginning of 2013 when **by chance I discovered the name of my "condition"**. A young grant holder set to work on my company and told me that during several days had experimented a detachment from the reality, like if he has seen everything as a dream, that he had searched on Google and that probably he could have suffered a disorder called "derealization". From that moment on everything changed. I got into the Internet and found out I would not be alone anymore. All the symptoms I'd been dealing with were similar to thousands and thousands of people, not only in Spain, but around the world as well.

From 2012 I began to suffer arterial hypertension, inherited from my father, so I had already acquired the habit of walking every evening for staying fit. It was **almost by accident I started to practice the mental exercises** I propose in chapter 7 to overcome my depersonalized state.

One given afternoon about November 2014, something amazing occurred. As any other afternoon I made big efforts to pay attention to the objects on the street and feel them as before, when I was 18 or 19 years old. While I was paying attention at the vivid colors of a semaphore through which I passed every day, **the green light of the pedestrian figure suddenly brought me back the memory of a toy of the same shade of green I had when I was a child**. It was as an electric connection, making my hair stood on end. It was thrilling and reassuring at the same time. It was the beginning of the end of my silent ordeal.

I was very touched, I wanted to cry at last and bec
my mind could come back to the normal state of th
the attack I suffered in 1988.

Words cannot describe enough what that experie

Connection came back suddenly while observing the green light of a semaphore

For the first time in 26 years and a half I felt something **had turned considerably for the better**. In the same way I suddenly disconnected myself many years ago I was connected again.

From this day on I was sure 'Santi' will come back to the real world, that boy whom **liked** chess, computers and the blue color. I knew my mind had got the most difficult thing, breaking the emotional deadlock existing for a long time and getting access to personal visual memories, to sensations, emotions. It was already a matter of time reassembling my personality.

Twenty six years and a half thinking with a mind dissociated are not easy to assimilate and normalize, but step by step, thanks to the exercises I put into practice **I could accustom my rational part to take again into account the emotional part step by step**. Once the field was clear I should be successful. That is the key to leave the depersonalization and derealization state, relaxing enough in order to listen to and feel again what we have stored in our emotional part and let it be important and relevant in our lives.

2   WHAT ARE THE SYMPTOMS OF DPDR DISSOCIATION?

Those who have just suffered this dissociation often complain about they feel that **SOMETHING HAS CHANGED IN THEIR MIND** and that they are not able to think normally as before. They feel detached from the world and start to think that maybe their life is a fake and that probably they are already dead, they see **the world as unreal and deceit**, that is like being on a stage where they are the main characters. They live in the third person like a spectator in their own lives. Symptoms of this dissociation, also called **feeling of unreality,** are very clear in the existing documentation.

There are two differentiated groups of symptoms which I describe this way:

Derealization (DR) consists of perceiving the world as unreal, as a dream, through a thick glass, distant, unattainable, grayer, flatter, more incomprehensible, different from the world we had lived so far. Like a film, something invisible as a transparent wall don't let us perceive the real world directly.

Depersonalization (DP) consists of not being able to find oneself, observing your face in a photograph and doubt about if that scene really happened or not, lacking goals or illusions in life, not feeling emotions and not having personal tastes, nor individual preferences. We cannot identify with our previous life before the disorder. We don't feel comfortable within our own body and doubt about our own existence.

DID YOU KNOW THAT...?

According to the fifth version of the Diagnostic and Statistical Manual of Mental Disorders (DSM-V) this disorder is called DDD

> *(Depersonalization/Derealization Disorder) and receives code number 300.6:*
>
> *DEREALIZATION: Unreality or detachment experiences respect to our environment (for instance individuals or objects are felt as unreal, dream-like sensation, in a fog, lifeless or visually distorted)*
>
> *DEPERSONALIZATION: Unreal/detachment experiences, of being an foreign spectator respect to our own thoughts, feelings, sensations, our body or actions (for instance, perceptive alterations, distorted sense of time, unreal or absent sense of the self, emotional and/or physical numbing)*

Patients typically have a combination of DP and DR, in this way there are people who complain that suffer more from DR than DP and vice versa, others assure they see the world normally and nevertheless feel strange to their selves.

I'll try to describe with my own words the sensation lived by dissociated people. Symptoms description is in line with the testimony of patients who suffered DPDR in the past or are still suffering it.

(I will use literal phrases on blue background to describe the symptoms from the people affected by this disorder)

The 'rare' state I lived in was **permanent**. Nothing could appease or alleviate it but sleep. That was clear for me. I slept a lot specially the first two years. That is a very common symptom during the first months or even years: **sleep and tiredness longer than normal**.

I will describe in more detail some of my main symptoms:

2.1   THE SENSE OF SIGHT

I saw things in a strange way, somehow blurry, but the most precise adjective was imperfect or uncompleted. Many testimonies talk about blurry vision, but probably because they cannot find a word which describes their strange visual perception they are experimenting. Despite being able to see everything and identify colors, objects and people who surrounded me, I felt I was not seeing ok. **Something was missing and I could not understand proper and quickly what I was seeing**. I perceived my parents and siblings as strangers although I knew they were my family and I should be accustom to see them. My house seemed strange too. I stared vacantly on many occasions, as if I could not focus well.

Everything seemed new, different, as if I see it for the first time. Like a scary movie!, don't you think? That got me nervous and confused me very much. To other people that sensation might have produced panic attacks and even think they were going mad, another frequent fear present in DPDR dissociation.

Sight is the main sense affected by DPDR

Despite distinguish between different colors as usual, the world seemed grayer to me. Colors DID NOT EVOKE ANY MEMORY OR EMOTION to me. I appreciated the coming of darkness time, since at least my state was more similar to normal state. The vision of the world was less confusing because there was nothing to see or at least I remained with my eyes closed.

I DID NOT UNDERSTAND literally the meaning of light, I could not understand the sky, so my sensation was worse while standing by open spaces or especially in front of natural landscapes. Nor I felt my hands as mine one hundred per cent. I could not process or understand the illumination of lamps over the objects, nor think about if there was light enough to develop some activity appropriately.

> *Juan Carlos I. (MÉXICO), 17 years old:*
>
> *"...supermarkets in my city are plenty of light, and light is something that depersonalized me excessively. It makes me believe my eyes cannot focus correctly objects or letters,..."*

I spent many hours in my room lying on my bed hearing music and I didn't want to do anything; after all **I did not exist, as if I was dreaming**. My existence could not influence anybody, I felt nothing I could do might have consequences for nobody and less for me.

The world seemed **flatter and deepless.** It was difficult to distinguish a particular object amongst others. It took me more time than normal seeking objects, requiring me certain effort. I hardly kept my eyes fixed over my body, arms or legs. And **seeing myself on the mirror was always hard and uncomfortable.** Who am I?, Where did I come from? , Have I existed before? ... Those were the questions I asked.

Social relationships are difficult while experiencing DPDR

In spite of recognizing familiar faces correctly, the fact of contemplating them makes me feel bad. I lost the skill of knowing **what should I do or feel when I meet someone**. Obviously It caused social withdrawal and apprehension to engage with others. If I barely knew who I was, how could I manage to treat the rest of people? Moreover, I could hardly remember my social and emotional life previous to the DPDR attack.

Difficulty in counting and grouping objects: The simple action of counting the number of persons in a room, **including myself**, it was too unclear. Surprisingly it was a task complicated for me. As if I was unable to include myself as another person in the count. I lost track very often and had to start again. It was hard to identify each person as an entity clearly differenced within the scene. In addition to that, the sensation of confusion was accentuated when contemplating determined repetitive visual patterns as mosaics or grids.

Difficulty in processing clearly the location of objects and my own body: I was incapable of place for my liking, my personal objects on my desk. I didn't care, its position was indifferent to me while they were all. When walking on the streets it was meaningless to me if I was placed in the middle of the pavement or close to the façade. I was sure I was walking careless and automatically, that I could hit someone at anytime. **I was unable to pay attention to those spatial aspects workaday**. We could say I walked robotically.

Difficulty in looking out for the details of things: I used to see just enough to identify the object or person. The way I shifted my gaze by objects it was different than normal. In some way it was slower and cumbersome. It was very hard for me turning my head from side to side to observe things.

Difficulty in perceiving adequately the size of things, including parts of my body**, or feeling the distance between myself and the rest of objects:** I felt like playing a role in a movie but not fully within it, just as a spectator of what my self was doing or saying.

Difficulty in assigning emotional meaning to different tones of the same color: It seemed there were just the basic colors: yellow, white, blue, beige, brown, green,... but I was not able to appreciate or evaluate different green, blue or any other tonality. Colors could not evoke anything from the past. As they suggested nothing to me, can you imagine my indecision when buying clothes...? What color to choose if I really hadn't any preference for anyone? It happened to me in many situations in life.

> **Lourdes J. 25 years old:**
>
> "...and noticed my eyesight and the feeling of my body had changed (I was sure I was not within it)... I was acting a role in a movie... as a machine ... I became hypochondriac and even suspected of having caught VIH..."
>
> **Iván A.R. (CHILE), 24 years old:**
>
> "...I feel very strange, when I stand up I feel everything rare , I asked myself questions such as how is that I can move my arms o why I walk automatically, I want to add that my eyesight is blurry and especially when I have to focus without my sunglasses which alleviate me a lot..."
>
> **Javier A.P. (MÉXICO), 28 years old:**
>
> "...I feel this is not my body, I feel trapped inside, in my eyesight all I can see is strange as if I was a passenger within a body that is not mine, sometimes I doubt who I am, well, I know it's me but I cannot feel me..."

2.2   THE SENSE OF HEARING

After suffering the derealization attack my sense of hearing was affected too. **I could hear and understand** conversations but it took me more time than normal to process them, **I used to hear the incoming sound as distant** and strange to me. I knew that physically my sense of hearing was well since I passed all the necessary audition tests to get my license driving or passing the yearly medical examination in my company. However I could not interpret easily the acoustic information which reached my ear.

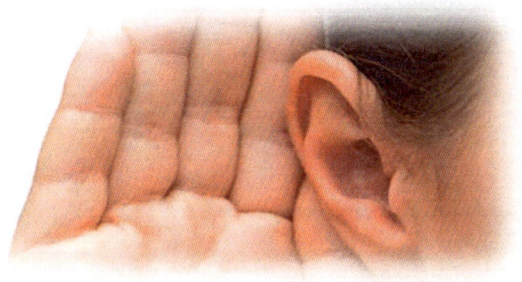

The sense of hearing is also affected

Main anomalies were:

Difficulty in recognizing my own voice: When I speak obviously I was aware it should be me who was talking, however I could not relate that sound completely to my self. It was as if I was aware that a part of me was speaking without being entirely me.

> *Layren M. A. (CUBA), 31 years old:*
>
> *"...I know it's my voice, it's logic, but I cannot feel it, so when I speak I also get very nervous as if I didn't know what gestures I should do with my face because I don't feel emotions, I do it in a logical way, faking even easy facial expressions. This is terrible!!*

Difficulty in estimating the volume (sound intensity): I used to doubt about if I speak too low or too high for my interlocutor. Nor I had a clear criterion to select the right volume in my equipment of music. I lacked sensitiveness enough to do that. I had lost my personal references in relation to if a determined sound was very high or very low.

Difficulty in capturing emotions transmitted in the tone of voice of other people: Although I could process the words pronounced by someone however I wasn't able to distinguish clearly if he was joking or if he was angry. It was confused to capture emotional details within conversations.

Because of the **remoteness** of the sounds reaching to my sense of hearing, **I didn't use to answer the first time** I was called in. I frequently asked again this way: *What have you said?,* although physically I have really heard the sound. I was numb.

In general **difficulty in hearing and processing sounds** produced by any object or person in the real world in a natural way: It required to me certain conscious effort. It seemed there was an intermediate barrier blocking the pathway to myself.

Sounds **could not evoke anything from my previous life**. However when I thought about which type of sound I was hearing, I succeed, but I could not understand them well. They generated to me confusion and a feeling of unease. Despite understanding the nature of the sound (i.e.: a bus passing, a dog barking,...) I could not relate them with my personal story. They seemed new.

I used to hum songs but most of the time without thinking consciously about the name of the singer or the song. In an automatic way, almost out-of-control **it entered into my head and it was hard to stop humming it.**

2.3   THE SENSES OF TOUCH, SMELL AND TASTE

I could not feel my hands as mine 100%. The same happened with the rest of my body. There was a certain separation between my thinking self and my body.

Intensity and variety of smells/flavors I could perceive **had clearly been decreased**. They did not remind me anything. I used to eat in a mechanical and unconscious way.

I did not pay adequate attention to the position of my body, hands, feet,... and I remember doing things in any way, carelessly.

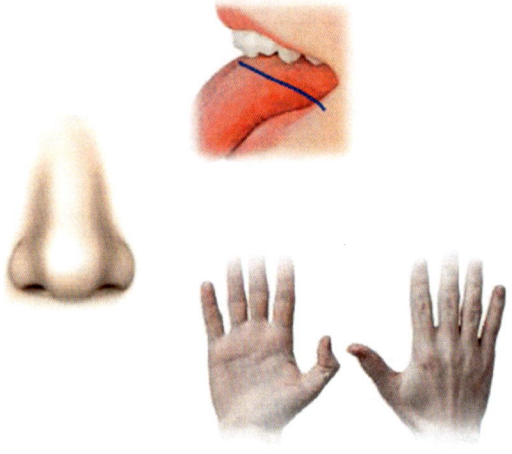

All senses are someway affected by DPDR

Sometimes I felt ungravity sensations, inability to feel my own weigh as I walked.

My senses were "numb" and the stimuli from the outside cushioned.

Even the internal senses of the body as **knowing when you are tired, hungry or sleepy, or noticing precisely the position of the body** were also affected.

2.4   ALTERED PERCEPTION OF TIME AND SPACE

While I was suffering derealization a simple look at a clock was cumbersome to me. I could not give a clear meaning to the lateness of the hour. Not that I could not say the hour the clock marked, I understood it, but **simply it didn't mean anything to me**. The same applied to every day of the week; **I didn't care if it was Saturday, Monday or Thursday**. I could feel nothing special. So why should I be glad for a Friday to come?

At the same time, I was not able to remind easily what had happened last week. I suffered certain difficulties to go back in time or planning what I should do next week, it was **as if I lived within an endless present**. In that way I could spend hours and hours focused on any issue and although I knew how many hours had passed simply looking at the clock, I didn't feel how much time had really gone by.

DPDR disorder induces an altered perception of time

In the first years of suffering DPDR I tried to hide and even putting upside-down the clocks at my parents' house because I could not cope with them. I preferred ignoring the time it was, I thought that was good for me. As far as that point this disorder can affect your day to day life.

An example of the inability of feeling the trace of time was that events happened a decade ago could be remembered as if they had happened only a week ago, and viceversa, a journey undertaken last week can be felt so far as if it had been many years ago.

> **Artal. C.R, (SPAIN), 21 years old:**
>
> *"...I don't have memory I can't remember the past, I can't remember the important events in my life, things that I should not be forgotten, I have lost track of time, days are passing and passing ..."*
>
> **Vicente T.P. (SPAIN), 23 years old:**
>
> *... nowadays I work as a personal trainer and physiotherapist ... my symptoms are difficulty in finding myself in time, planning,...*

Routinely, for these 26 years, I noticed **I had trouble to find my orientation** or remembering from which entrance I had entered a car park or where I had left my car parked on the street, or where I might have left the keys of my home. I looked for them at normal places and finally I found them, of course, but never reliving my movements around the house until seeing where I left them. I applied **logic**, but I could not remind the images captured by my eyes.

"Time distortion" illustrated by Eloy T.C. (SPAIN), 26 years old

2.5   THE MEMORY

After suffering my attack of permanent DPDR, my ability to read and study collapsed. Mi ability to focus was reduced significantly and my academic performance as a student of a university career fall to a 10% of what could have been.

It was if as the new content I read could not be fit anywhere. As if my brain had "hanged" or "overloaded" and could not assimilate anything more until it had digested the huge binge of concepts I had. Telecommunication engineering was **a continuous succession of new information of rational type to be comprehended** and assimilated in a very short time**.**

However, five years later I started to read texts good enough and more easily and **without knowing very well how**, I began to prepare subjects of my engineering and passing them successfully. Anyhow, I stayed in an unreal haze that leaded me a great insecurity and objectively undermined my academic skills. In fact, **it was surprising that I was be able to pass subjects,** though I did, **because I forced myself to sit my exams although always ignoring if I was adequately prepared**.

People affected by DPDR **cannot assess how much knowledge they have** and that produces a lot of insecurity. They lack the necessary global perspective to do that.

Since the day of the DPDR attack I ceased remembering easily what I have done during the last week ot the last month,…, and I could not access to episodes of my own life. I could remember data, dates, names of persons I had known, but they were blank, they meant nothing to me, it was strange, wasn't it? Moreover, **I could not visualize them in any concrete place** when thinking of them. Somehow my "biographic memory "was partially affected too.

> **Antonio L. (SPAIN), 24 years old:**
>
> "..time goes by and I am absent... I have memory problems, especially with in the short-term,... I certainly notice a significant detachment from current reality. I feel my head is blank, as numb, as if I was a zombie"
>
> **Andrés T. C. (SPAIN), 23 years old:**
>
> "I feel absolutely unable to use my memory... I am living the days as if they were nothing, I don't have illusion, even as if I don't exist. I am trying to think and I cannot, I am blocked permanently"
>
> **Tania E. C. (MEXICO), 24 years old:**
>
> "...I am still wondering why I am feeling this way, because although I am trying to go on with my life there is something that prevents me for doing so. I am afraid of losing my memory, that I will get asleep and won't remember anything when I wake up, I cannot work because i am getting in and out from reality..."

In addition to the above **it was very confused to pay attention and learn the rules of any new game**. I could play reasonably well those I had already learnt before the attack, but I avoid the new ones. I was always **afraid of misunderstanding their rules**. Also I could not enjoy from them as before. I still remember how it was before having DPDR, I enjoyed opening the box of new board games, I read and understood quickly their rules, particularly I remember well the game called "RISK", the game consisting on conquering the world, one of the last games I learnt before the attack. I enjoyed so much learning to play it, and even more with the dynamism of this game. Once I fell into the DPDR I stopped playing this type of games completely.

2.6 NO ACCESS TO PERSONAL HISTORY AND EXISTENCIAL QUESTIONS

When I fell into derealization it was as if I was cut off, suddenly severed from my **personal** memories. All 'normal' people saves a record of **when and where** have got their successes, their personal items, their experiences, their adventures, their friends, their contacts,…, what it is called 'biographic memory'. Also they have a place where keep everything is pending, their favorite activities remaining to be done, friends to be called, etc…, **suddenly I lost a clear access to the things to be done, to any illusion or goal.**

A person suffering DPDR lacks a self. Difficult to explain to any person had never experienced it. A DPDR person feels himself **hollow, blank, mere window-dressing,** feels **as a robot** which is still living but it doesn't know how or for what. Somewhat as a 'living dead' or 'zombie' and having deep, philosophical, repetitive, circular thoughts as… Who am I?, Why do I exist?, Do they exist too?, Will everything be a dream?, If I was not here, never mind as I cannot feel anything, I am blank as a ghost!! Why can't I end all this suffering?

> *Anonymous, 12/02/2016*
>
> *"…I wonder what the world is, what the universe is, what a person is, who I am, I am a human being, I am a woman, why I am a woman, why people are as they are, why we have hands, eyes, why an object is as it is, who create it, how it works, what the time is, whether the time exists,… I can't understand why I doubt about the nature of things, about people or about who I am, how it can be I feel stranger to my self, how I can questioned all this, how it can be that if I know exactly how it's all today I feel everything strange, I cannot understand why I can doubt of everything and concluding nonsenses as the world does not exist, I am not exist or I am not who I am'*

A person with DPDR is aware more or less about **what** has done throughout his life, but he **cannot** visualize clearly with images **when**

or where, he can hardly remember dates, people's names ... It's confusing. This is because he lacks a global view about who he is.

> ***Erik H., (MÉXICO), 22 years old:***
>
> *"...I cannot look to the past nor imagine the future, somehow my memories don't seem as mine and are emotionless, as if I was disconnected from myself, as if my identity had been erased and had lost the track of time. Really I don't find any motivation and I can hardly go to work..."*

2.7   EMOTIONS, PREFERENCES AND DECISION MAKING

Another devastating symptom of my depersonalization was the **lack of emotions**, inability to feel love or sorrow as before the attack. For instance, I could reason that in a determined situation I should feel pain as in very sad occasions like the death of a close relative. I was completely aware that it could be a very painful situation, but I was unable to really feel it.

It's very common to stop feeling emotions when suffering DPDR

For 26 years I could not shed a single tear. My thoughts **were not able to strike any emotional chord**. First years were very difficult and many times I thought why don't end all. I believed it would have been logical to burst into tears since this situation was very sad and desperate for me. Despite knowing it, crying was almost physically impossible to me. There was no connection to my emotional side.

Colors and shapes of things meant nothing to me, I could not decide which color tone of a shirt or the color of a car I liked best. Why?, because my SELF was missing. I was a thinking being who could remember the names of everything but **was unable to feel any personal bias**. In this way, **any option was good**, for instance, when going out with friends and I had to choose a restaurant or a cocktail bar. I let myself go. I didn't care. I molded to anything. Someone might think that was an advantage. While it was true **I suffered for nothing, it was always true I did not enjoy for anything**. Was that a life?

When taking decisions my problems were overwhelming. I used to 'procrastinate', to delay decisions as long as possible. All my criteria were logic and none of them based on emotions. I was not sure to take decisions good for ME. When I doubted due to not feeling if a decision suited me, I always put up the prudence and compiling data before 'making a move'.

"If you don't know where you're going, any road will take you there"

A clear example of the difficult situations I faced was choosing a gift for someone. Since I lacked an emotional connection it was not easy to find out what would interest most to the birthday boy/girl or on an anniversary. I used to recall what had already bought in other occasions and my criterion was logic/rational. There was no place for 'crazy things' or 'going overboard'. The rationale was my only inner compass.

> *Rosvita M.A, (CHILE), 38 years old:*
>
> '...it's as if I don't exist, I have trouble making decisions because **I don't know what is the right way** and that's why it's getting more difficult, furthermore I have a lot of memory loss '
>
> *Esmeralda C.H, (MÉXICO), 19 years old:*
>
> "...some days I have that sensation as if everything had lacked any sense at all, as if I don't belong to the world and things that, before having DPDR, made me happy when thinking or recalliing **don't make me feel anything. I can't feel emotions as before when I was normal**'
>
> *Fran V., (ESPAÑA), 18 years old:*
>
> "My symptoms are: numbness in my head, I can't hardly think, I find so difficult memorizing and however previously to the attack I had good memory, I could remind things from my nursery when I was 4. Now I can't remember recent events, my memories are emotionless,... another symptom is time,... My feelings about my love ones are as clouded... for instance with my couple: **I know I love her but I cannot feel it in my heart...**'

2.8   SOCIAL BEHAVIOUR

What a normal social behavior can have a person that cannot have in mind his own existence, that cannot find himself, that ignores his preferences, that doesn't know where he is going, no aims, unable to remember what he did in the past, that cannot feel, that sees everything rare, remote, feeling everything as new although be known, that doesn't end up feeling ok with his own body, that when speaking it seems another person is emitting the sound, not him, that he's amazed at what he says in any moment, that when someone tells him the rules of a new game he cannot process them properly, that he feels so bad in open spaces typical on trips, that when look at the clock gets nervous because he cannot understand well how many things can do in a time period and so many other functional disruptions.

SO HE FEELS BAD, INSECURE, QUIET AND PARTICIPATING THE LEAST POSSIBLE.

Spontaneity fully disappeared after be derealized. The more informal and freewheeling was a meeting of friends the WORSE. The more formal and specific to a topic for discussion or business issue the BETTER.

An example of the worse conceivable scene was, let's say, an excursion to the field in a cloudy day (under the typical diffused gray light) in order to play, sing songs or telling jokes. With nothing concrete to do, JUST FEELING, MAKING RELATIONSHIPS AND DEVELOPING CREATIVE ACTIVITIES. That sounded to me as *'Buf!, the hell on earth, I want to go away right now, go back home to the solitude of my room'.* To tell you the truth, before 20 years old I didn't like those situation either, I used to be uncomfortable, nervous, a hard time for me even lacking any mental disorder yet.

Estefanía O. P. (SPAIN), 32 years old:

*"... the next day when I woke up everything had changed. I relied on it will leave by itself, but no way... days progressed and I remained the same. I didn't want to leave from home, I felt horrible outside, I was **losing my relations.***

Manuela G. V. (COLOMBIA), 15 years old:

*"...that feeling of not knowing who I was, **that all even family and friends were strange for me**, it's very difficult remember my previous life, as if I didn't have any feeling, I can't feel, it's desperate.*

3   UNDERSTANDING OUR BRAIN A LITTLE BIT

In this third chapter I will try to set the basis of my hypothesis about the nature of the DPDR disorder. There is certain brain zone, between rational and emotional minds which is affected by the dissociation. Nowadays I still ignore the exact location and the specific elements of the brain where the disconnection between both minds takes place. All the evidences lead us to determine that that impairment or loss of communication can origin all the typical symptoms, specially the unreality of the self (Depersonalization) as well as world unreality (Derealization).

Of course this is only a plausible hypothesis, and any medical professional who could be reading these lines should not trust directly from the opinion of persons who are not members of his/her profession, however at the same time he should at least begin a research project about it since it comes from another scientist and who has got first-handed knowledge about this dissociation for more than 25 years.

Once I fell in permanent depersonalization I decided **to learn by myself about brain structure and about memory**. In 1988, without Internet, research was reduced to go to libraries or to buy specialized books. I bought two books, the first one called 'Left brain/right brain' (by Sally P.Springer and Georg Deustch) and another one about learning and memory (by Donald A.Norman).

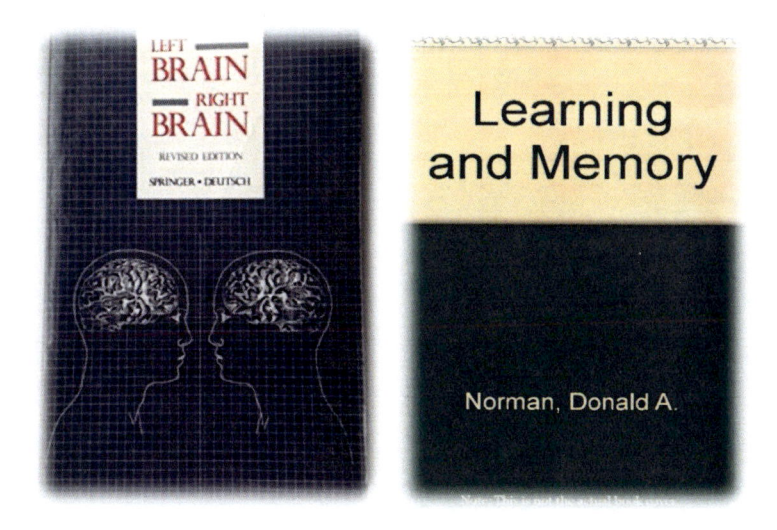

Two books I bought in 1989 trying to find out what had happened to my mind

Thanks to these readings and my technical background as Telecommunication engineer I could establish, twenty years after, my own hypothesis about DPDR nature and to understand why my method based on determine cognitive exercises was working.

Human brain is divided in two hemispheres clearly separated but connected mainly by the corpus callosum, a relatively little set of nervous connections that joins them. **Each hemisphere is specialized naturally** in different functions.

3.1 LEFT HEMISPHERE OF BRAIN

Left hemisphere is specialized in written and spoken language. Mathematical abstractions, symbols and concepts are also store here. It's our **rational** mind, the syllogisms one, it's our inner voice, that mind who asks questions. Definitely it is our consciousness.

Left brain likes **rules**, procedures, order, **sequence** and the processes.

Left hemisphere has an **encyclopedic and deductive memory**. It is in charge of controlling the conscious actions of human beings.

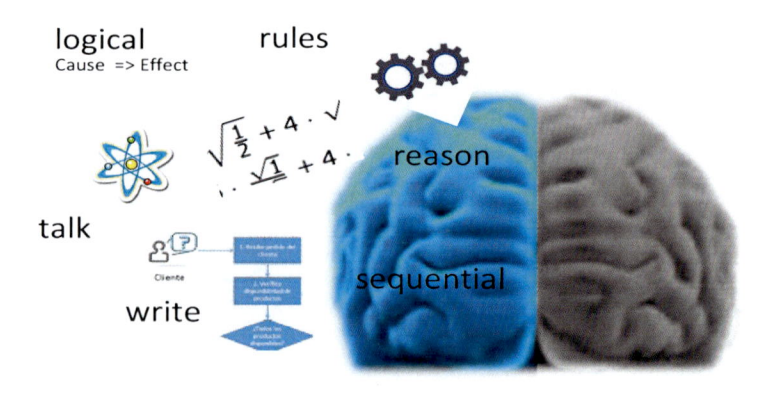

Our SELF, the one thinking with words is placed at the left hemisphere

It houses **our logical mind, the mind of reason.** It's the philosophical mind, the one able to ask transcendent questions.

Traditional educational model of schools and universities gives priority to minds which left hemispheres are more perfect and tends to perpetuate its development. From the early days everybody must respect hundreds of norms at school. There are checkpoints, exams, where there is only a right answer to every exercise.

Left hemisphere speaks to us but it is **unable to feel emotions**, since that is land of the right hemisphere and its strong connection with the limbic system.

Speaking about the motor development, left hemisphere controls the right side of our body, including the right visual field.

3.2 RIGHT HEMISPHERE OF BRAIN

The right hemisphere is specialized on **patterns recognition**. It is mute but it's **connected with emotions** (much more connected with hippocampus and amygdale than the left hemisphere). We are talking about **it has more to do with the limbic system**.

It is equipped with a memory based on **images**. It works on parallel at high speed with information not necessary completed. For example, it is in charge of the indispensable facial recognition.

It is the hemisphere of the **art, colors, innovation and creativity.** It is also the hemisphere which register and qualify emotionally all the events we have experienced in the past.

It is the hemisphere of real objects and examples of the real world. It is the hemisphere which can process **images in 3D** (three dimensions). It provides **deepness** and distance calculations.

It can **instantly** evaluate a situation **in a holistic way** (**complete**) and provide a general and emotional judgment of it.

The right hemisphere manages space, time, body, senses, emotions...

Since it can access to our personal history stored somewhere in the **hippocampus** it's able to manage our habits and customs. It helps us to give **personal meaning** to everything we do workaday.

According to the locomotive system the right hemisphere controls the left side of our body, including the left visual field.

Normal 'persons' use naturally and indistinctly functions of both hemispheres when needed since they are **connected directly by a set of nerves called 'corpus callosum' and indirectly by other paths**.

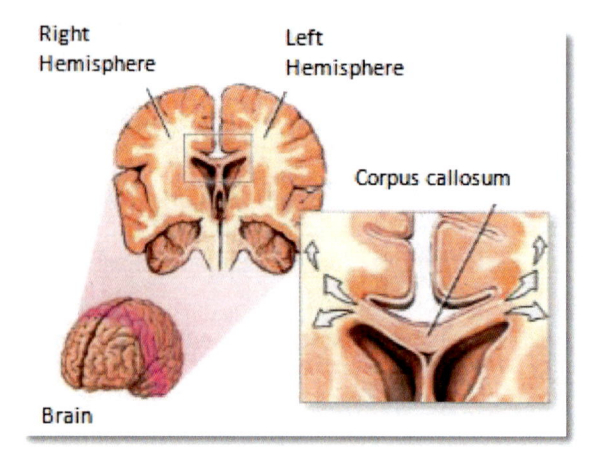

The connection between both hemispheres

As a curiosity, when I say 'person', who am I referring to? Thus the thinking mind of a human being, to his consciousness, to that being able to asking questions as...

Where did I leave the keys to my home?

That thinking being it is located basically in the left hemisphere of your brains.

I am sure you can remember from the time you were still ok these two approaches to find those keys:

1. **Thinking logically** in which parts of my house I have stepped and looking in common places where I use to leave them.
2. A visual approach. Reviewing as a film what I have done since I entered the house. **Seeing through which places stepped and what I did with my hands** after opening the front door.

Approach #1 corresponds to absent-minded people, absorbed in their thoughts, it can take long time and it's in charge of the rational left hemisphere.

Approach #2 belongs to sensitive people, opened up to the world, very active in their right hemisphere. It's the quicker approach as long as we 'have recorded' consciously those movements. It can only be done by the 'visual' hemisphere, the right one.

3.3   SOME RELIABLE SCIENTIFIC SOURCE

Although the perspective of this book is not scientific, but autobiographical and self-helping, I cannot resist mentioning and exposing some fragments of **at least one current reliable source** which supports my hypothesis:

Allan N. Schore is a doctor in clinical psychiatric who has been studying for two decades about the early trauma on brain development and the relationship between the emotional right hemisphere and the subconscious self.

Dr. Alan N. Schore, from Los Angeles University (UCLA) studies right hemisphere influence in the SELF

www.allanschore.com

He is author of several books as 'The science of the art of psychotherapy' or 'Affect regulation and the origin of the self', also he use to publish and review scientific papers in the most prestigious magazines of psychology and psychiatry.

Among his numerous articles we can mention some recent as:

    I.   *'The Right Brain Implicit Self: A Central Mechanism of the Psychotherapy Change Process', 2016*

    II.   *'Early Right Brain Development: How love opens creativity, play and Arts', in press*

    III.   *'Dysregulation of the right brain: a fundamental mechanism of traumatic attachment and the psychopathogenesis of posttraumatic stress disorder', 2014*

    IV.   *'Right brain affect regulation', 2009*

    V.   ...

*In the next scheme, **extremely important** in my view to understand the nature of DPDR, which appearing in several of those articles and books can be clearly shown the connection between the rational mind (to the left, **language** oriented) and the emotional mind (to the right, ruled by **images** and sensations) and how the limbic system, in charge of motivation and emotions is strongly linked to the right hemisphere and too far away from our rational SELF.*

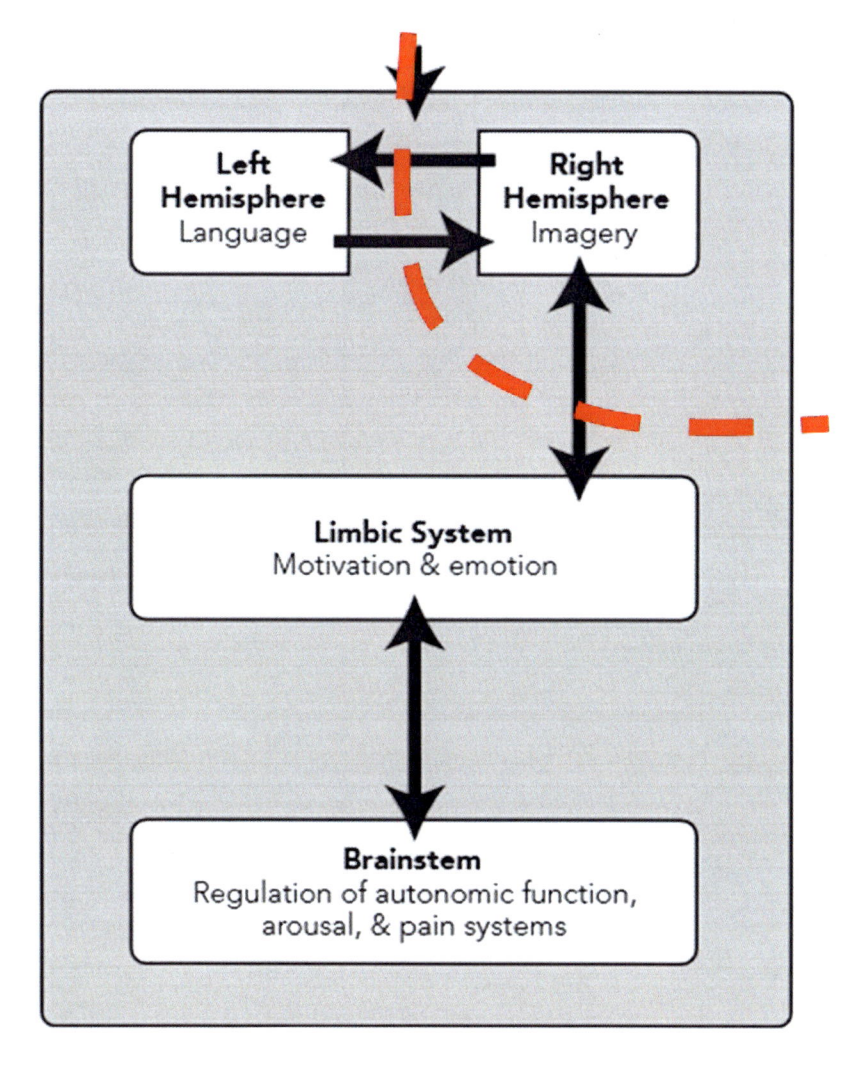

[Diagram: Box containing Left Hemisphere (Language) and Right Hemisphere (Imagery) connected by arrows at top; both connecting down to Limbic System (Motivation & emotion); which connects down to Brainstem (Regulation of autonomic function, arousal, & pain systems). A dashed red line curves through the diagram separating the right hemisphere area.]

The dashed red line, added by me, indicates the zone where the disconnection could have happened

I mention here several assertions scientifically proven about the right hemisphere that can be found in the first article of the above list:

- *'The concept of a single unitary SELF is as misleading as the idea of a single unitary brain. The left and right hemispheres process information in their own unique fashions, and this is reflected in a conscious left lateralized self system (left mind) and an unconscious right lateralized self system (right mind)'* [Page 178]

- *'The more diffuse organization of the right hemisphere has the effect that it responds to any stimulus, even speech stimuli, **more quickly** and, thus earlier. The left hemisphere is activated after this and performs the slower semantic analysis... The right hemisphere operates a distributed network for rapid responding to danger and other urgent problems. It preferentially process environmental challenge, stress and pain and manages self-protective responses as avoidance and escape.... Emotionally is thus the right brain's red phone, compelling the mind to handle urgent matters without delay.* [Page 179]

- *'I describe a surface, verbal, conscious, analytic explicit self versus a deeper non-verbal, non-conscious, holistic, emotional corporeal implicit self. These two lateralized systems contain qualitatively different forms of cognition and therefore ways of 'knowing' as well as different memory systems and states of consciousness.* [Page 181]

- *'... the left hemisphere is dominant for language but the right is dominant for emotional communication'* [Page 182]

- *'... the definition of intuition, the ability to understand or know something immediately, without conscious reasoning (Compact Oxford English Dictionary), clearly implies right and not left brain processing'* [Page 183]

- *' The emerging picture from the current literature seems to suggest a special role of the right hemisphere in **self-related***

> cognition, own body perception, self-awareness and autobiographical memories' [Page 185]

- '... the phenomenon of **dissociation as a defense** against SELF destabilization [Page 188]

- '**Autobiographical memory, an output of the right brain**, is the highest memory system that consists of **personal events with a clear relation to time, space, and context**. [Pages 195-196]

It is worth to highlight other assertions from the fourth article listed above:

- '... later-forming reaction to relational trauma is dissociation, in which the child disengages from stimuli in the external world – traumatized infants are observed to be staring off into space with a glazed look ... **The dissociative metabolic shutdown state is a primary regulatory process, used throughout the lifespan, in which the stressed individual passively disengages** in order to conserve energies... etc... [Page 120]
- At all points of the lifespan, dissociation is conceptualized as 'a basic part of the psychobiology of the human trauma response: a protective activation of altered states of consciousness in reaction to overwhelming psychological trauma'. [Pages 121-122]
- 'If children grow up with dominant experiences of separation, distress, fear and rage, then they will go down a bad pathogenic developmental pathway, **and it's not just a bad psychological pathway but a bad neurological pathway**' [Page 123]
- ...

There are many more references within the work of Dr Allan Schore, however he doesn't seem to refer to DPDR disorder specifically at any *moment. In my hypothesis and seemingly within his work,* **after a point of no return, the brain evolves from a hyperactive state due to stress, anxiety, fear, or trauma to a passive and dissociated state when there have been produced neurologic and biochemical major changes.** *Departing from a problem which can be psychologically treated it becomes a neuro-chemical and psychological problem.*

The conclusion is that the patient, despite efforts, becomes completely powerless to think normally again. **The insurmountable wall he feels that separate him from his body and from his emotions is a real wall and is not merely psychological.** *A new approach is required instead of the standard treatment against anxiety.*

Since the right hemisphere becomes shielded and gets isolated from the left hemisphere as well as from the rest of limbic system is totally understandably the huge set of different symptoms which the patient suddenly experiments during a DPDR attack.

4   WHAT IS CONSCIOUSNESS?

The DPDR disorder consists of an altered state of consciousness, is the result of mind dissociation.

I have already mentioned that I am a telecommunication engineer, not a psychologist nor a psychiatrist or neurologist but I have performed a great and forced introspection of my mind during many years I experienced DPDR. My perspective is not medical in nature although if there is any medical professional reading these lines it would be fine if he/she could contact me to share points of view about DPDR:

(*santos.barrioscanseco@gmail.com*)

The human being has a nervous system commanded by his brain, being able to action our organs in an automatic way (as the heart), semi-automatic way (when breathing) or on a voluntary basis (for instance when you move your hand or when you say something).

Consciousness, <u>for me</u>, is a mental state that let us to perceive and react to the world according to our personality (goals, experiences, preferences, beliefs …), and to take decisions that move us to action or to reflection. It might mean a 'process' which is active while we are awake. At night, our brain is accessed by unconscious process that, according to different sources, is set to perform the necessary maintenance tasks and consolidation of information acquired during the day.

Ingesting chemical substances can alter the normal functioning of the consciousness (alcohol, drugs …), that is widely recognized.

What kind of information uses a normal consciousness at any moment?

- It retrieves information from **internal sensors** of temperature, pain, digestive system,… (am I cold or hot?, am I ok?, is any part of my body pains me?, have I discomfort or sick due something I have eaten?, should I go to the bathroom?,..) as well as from the clothes I wear on my body.

- It stores a record of **where we are** (workplace, home, cinema …) and **in which position** is the body over its environment. *For instance, reminding that when we are in an attic room we should be careful with our head and avoid hitting the ceiling.*

- It analyses the **information from the situation and position of our body as well as the rest of objects**, persons, animals and other obstacles which may constitute a potential danger to our health. It calculates the right distance to orient itself respect to them

- It analyses the amount of **light** that enters the eye and:

    o It judges **if it is enough or not in order to develop a determined activity** taking into account past similar experiences.

    o It evaluates if the source of **light is external or internal**. In the case it decides it's external it can estimate an approximated hour of the day. It also take into account the **season** to calculate that hour (depending of the place as well). The length of the shadows projected by the sun it's info unconsciously stored and processed to do that estimation. That unconscious information together with the reading of the current time and the access to habits and hourly customs during all our life will guide us to know if we are getting late or not, if we need to have a break to rest during an activity, how long we are with it, etc…

DPDR generates problems to process and understand the light

- o It turns/move the body position in some way the cast shadow doesn't impede the activity to be completed.
- **It analyses the sound collected** (music, voices, chirping of birds, noise of trains,…) and determines if it is normal or not. If it should ignore it, just passing or if that is an anomalous sound that can pose a potential danger.
- It analyses the information from the rest of senses (touching, smelling and taste) which could evoke negative or positive past experiences.
- It has **in mind some pending activities which bring it pleasure** and when it finishes its duties it would like to put into practice.
- **It scans all important people in his recent life (couple, children, parents, siblings, friends …)** and keeps in mind the state of the relationship with them. Am I angry or not with some of them? When did I see them for the last time? At the same time it **self-evaluates its own emotional state** and determines which actions he might do in near future with each of them.

- It accesses and consciously handles **visual information** stored in the right hemisphere fostering creativity and innovation by mixing images. It can access to images from the past and recreate possible images to the future.

- It accesses to a **record of pending obligations**: Have I anything pending? From who? Is it priority? Must I have to react now? How much time is available to me to perform it?

- **It accesses and handles conceptual information stored permanently in the left hemisphere** (words, assertions, syntaxes, formula, data, processes, rules…) **to solve or doing problem statements,** learning new concepts,… For example, that occurs when we read a book, while we study or when we have a conversation with somebody.

As you can imagine, the partial disconnection originated by DPDR affects permanently to a proper perception of oneself and the world. It mainly affects to the consciousness since everything related with **the body, the senses, time, space and emotions** is involved.

5   FREQUENT CAUSES. WHY DOES IT HAPPEN?

MY HIPOTHESIS OF WEAK CONNECTION BETWEEN RATIONAL MIND AND EMOTIONAL MIND

Can you recall the symptoms I experienced? What could have produced so many symptoms abruptly? The day I suffered the permanent depersonalization attack **I felt as a disconnection inside my brain**. As if a cable had been unplugged inside and as a consequence I had lost basically (1), my ability of perceiving the world properly, (2) the access to my own personality, MY SELF and (3) the access to my emotions and personal history.

A graphic analogy of how can be produced the sudden disconnection between The rational and the emotional mind

Under my point of view, based on the existing documentation, hundreds of testimonials from depersonalized/derealized persons, my relative knowledge about brain and my own insights and feelings experienced for the long twenty six years of permanent DPDR I can establish that:

>A) Left and right hemisphere of the brain are connected basically by a limited number of nerves located in the corpus callosum.

B) The thinking SELF, the one that leads the thought and able to ask questions is placed in the left hemisphere and uses words. Concretely it is placed in the 'Left Prefrontal Cortex'.

C) The right hemisphere is connected with the hippocampus much more than the left one. The latter is in charge of store our personal history. It is connected with the right amygdala, the little organ that links thoughts and emotions (it can process images, sounds, touching stimuli ...)

D) Our consciousness, a mental process in charge of perceiving the world and responsible for taking decisions, uses the logical part as well as the emotional one in a normal person. It is altered by the DPDR so much that the patient could believe is going to fall into madness anytime.

I have reached the reasonable assumption that **the physical cause that origins the characteristic symptoms of DPDR is a <u>weak or deficient neural communication between both hemispheres, the logical one and the emotional one</u>**. This lack of communication produces the unpleasant sensation of having lost something important as the soul or the vital spark, the unpleasant sensation of having lost the SELF. Each hemisphere works fine but separately, they don't communicate between them as before. It's as there were two SELVES, the one thinking of words and the other one which controls and moves the body. I am oversimplifying the complex functioning of our brain, but in general that is the explanation **of feeling observed by ourselves**, seeing everything in third-person view, feeling robotic, without controlling what we say or how we move and so many symptoms as you can read in chapter 2.

Why that communication path has been weakened/atrophied?

i. By ingesting **substances** which disturb the normal chemistry of our brain: marihuana, LSD, hallucinogenic mushrooms, ayahuasca, and certain medicaments as benzodiazepines...
ii. When suffering a **great emotional trauma** (serious automobile accidents, sexual abuses, sudden and

unexpected death of a relative who we had a great dependency on, a sudden move to an hostile environment, new customs and habits, etc....). Symptom of PTSD (Post-Traumatic Stress Disorder).

iii. Due to suffer an **stressful situation and anxiety for a long time** (my own story)

In case number i., there are many testimonials of patients who ensure that just a single dose of marihuana led them to enter into a depersonalization/derealization state.

Smoking marihuana over a basis of stress or generalized anxiety disorder can generate DPDR

In case number ii, depersonalization comes from the self-protecting goal of our brain over our own negative emotions. **Brain cuts the link between the logical and emotional part to overcome the extreme experienced situation**, more than a normal human being can bear. That reaction, in principle acceptable and reasonable turns to be a chronic disease when that communication path cannot be reestablished by itself.

In case number iii, the individual himself, by his anxiety to achieve his purpose and his high stress level leads to consciously neglect the information provided by his right hemisphere since he **has more**

important concerns than making a balance of his life, being conscious of his emotions or paying attention to what surrounds him. He is focused on his generating anxiety issue and **step by step the connection was weakening until reach a point of no return**. The individual consciously ignores and misses the neural connection between rational and emotional part, which ends up weakening because of the lack of use till it is almost impracticable.

In any case it is important to distinguish the root cause which produced the DPDR, normally **a strong anxiety or stress** from the concrete stimulus which triggered it (drugs, emotional trauma, sudden change of vital environment, hostile situation, …)

6 LIVING WITHOUT EMOTIONAL COMPONENTS

A depersonalized person is completely aware of his limitations and the situations which increase his unreality sensation.

A depersonalized person lives without perceiving adequately **time, space, emotions, the complete scope of the situations, without goals and hardly knowing who is** him or if he is a real person.

The day starts with **the awakening**, a different awakening from a normal person. When a normal person is aware that he's already up, rapidly **retrieves mentally what he was dealing with**, what left pending the night before and gets up with vitality to finish up or start his daily duties or interests. On the contrary a person with DPDR awakes and **cannot feel any objective to be accomplished**, any desire to be fulfilled, or any wishful thinking to get up.

*For instance, if it is a holiday he will look at the bed clock, 8:42 am, and won't find any reason to continue sleeping or on the contrary getting up. He will doubt. He will know the **time should be passing, as always, however he cannot feel it**.* Look at the clock again, 8:55 am. Thirteen minutes have passed, but he cannot feel if it is long or short time to remain on bed. Finally, and in an automatic way ends up getting up (he knows people use to get up at any given time) with a lost look, being unable to focus anything concrete and ignoring if he did it in the appropriate time.

Wake up time is a very unpleasant moment for a DPDR person

Living with DPDR is self-observing and being amazed about what we do and say. Permanent dissociation between both cerebral zones, rational and emotional, generates the sensation of being observed constantly by your own thoughts. **Oneself is never sure about the speech or action be appropriate to each occasion**, he's always concealing before the rest of people that everything is ok, although really is not.

DPDR is more than just an unpleasant and horrific sensation, it represents an impairment, **a real decrease of our brain abilities**. Therefore, living with that it's a continuous fight to compensate missing functions by means of your own rational power.

A healthy and awakened mind needs the contribution of both planes, logical and emotional to work with full capacity. There are so many daily situations that require a proper emotional intelligence that it's not strange that the way of being of DPDR people can be affected. **In addition to the emotional deficit the individual suffers different secondary functional effects** due to the disconnection:

- Overall **slowing** to understand global situations. Over time, due to the absence of global vision, it appears the tendency to make schemes of situations or problems and to collect certain data about each situation. The lack of bird's eye-view is replaced by exhaustiveness.

- **Confusion** around scenario with a great number of stimuli, it is hard to group and classify.
- Difficulty and slowness when **taking decisions**. Aspects of the decisions are not clearly seen or felt.
- Energy and willingness lost to make thinks. There are no goals in life anymore. **There is no a previous SELF who has to continue** anything.
- Everything seems gray and strange and that sensation together with the impossibility of overcoming the disorder can easily lead the patient to a depressed mood.
- **Difficulty to focus**, eyes are heavy and anchored on fixed spots. Blank stare is very common. Inability to feel and take into account the distance between the body and the rest of the objects.
- **Difficulty to process determined complex or repetitive visual patterns.** The mere contemplation of the branches of a tree, the ground or the sky is confusing and increase the unreality sensation. Our rational hemisphere simply cannot manage the huge number of visual information, not logical, existing in these scenes.

There are many NO RATIONAL stimuli in a landscape or at the perfumery zone in a supermarket

- **Difficulty to process faces** in order to evaluate the emotional state of other people. Also inability to understand the emotional relationship **among different persons** within a group. The individual feels isolated from the group.
- Tendency to ruminate logical and philosophical recurrent thoughts. **Everything should have a logic explanation for a people suffering DPDR**. That fact origins frustration since the individual cannot process and understand all the items in the world and understand the meaning of his own existence. Trying to understand EVERYTHING *it's simply overwhelming and exhausting*. Existing and be borne is illogical since someday we will die. The fact there are other persons with their own lives cannot be process as well. *Aren't they a product of my mind?*
- Decrease in capacity about remembering past space-time aspects as well as projecting situations towards the future.
- Inability to feel correctly the **trace of time** which generates consternation
- The **limit between the body and the world** is not clearly distinguished.
- Lack of spontaneity, etc.

In definitive, living without a proper access to the space-temporal plane turns **the individual in a logic robot dealing with the enormous challenge** of controlling **a life he knows must be his but cannot identify with**. Despite this fact he keeps certain data about his origins and logically tries to follow the adequate way path he should travels, in autopilot mode, dissembling, **maintaining before oneself and the others that that body which is walking by it's still his**.

It's a true puzzle and a great mess for those have never experienced this hard dissociation.

I assure you from personal experience that **it's very, very exhausting that sensation of having to control a life from the control booth**.

Habitual sensation of being observed from oneself coming from the disconnection between both minds

Living with DPDR is as if you live permanently with a little dizziness or drunkenness, 'stoned' or whatever you call it, in an altered state of consciousness. For those normal people are reading these lines, I ask you: **How would you feel if after having drunk a little, being dizzy and going to bed hoping this sensation disappears you'd be awaken** with **THE SAME SENSATION OF CONFUSION?** How did you describe your state? Would you be able to lead a normal life? How would you feel after several weeks, months or even years with that confusion? What kind of explanation would you give to the people around you about this 'inability'? Would you be able to study, work, or maintain a relationship in that dizzy state? In the same way an inebriated person is aware he is not ok, a person with DPDR **is fully conscious about his rareness** and the only thing he desires is to be cured as soon as possible to continue with his life.

'It is as a great parenthesis had been opened in life.

People with DPDR miss desperately their former SELF'

Since I could live that awakening, that closing parenthesis, I can tell you that in fact, **I spent all those years waiting to be MYSELF again in order to relive**. Meanwhile, I did what I could to avoid mistakes and make reasonable decisions, but it's as if I hadn't lived a hundred percent, completely, all the situations I lived for so long. I couldn't make them mine.

Despite I knew everything I had done, good or bad, during all those years, I couldn't assimilate to my personality. As if my personality was hibernating in a *'stand-by'* state. **Nothing happened to me that affected me personally**. Only now I begin to **really understand, to notice, what I have lived** and to incorporate it to my personal story, that story truncated in April, 1988.

I lived 26 years without be completely conscious about what I did and the importance of that actions to ME. Now is time of rewinding and processing what happened to me emotionally. It is time of astonishment and strong emotions.

hemispheres, right hemisphere activation exercises ... and, naturally, the set of exercises specifically designed by me to treat DPDR that will be presented below.

I hope the same I did could be helpful to escape from the unreal state in which you are living now. You must remember that my case is the one of a person living with *depersonalization and derealization for* more than 25 years and caused by a prolonged stressful/anxiety situation. The more similar my case and yours be, the greater probability it works fine for you.

Every case **requires a personalized approach** and in any way I have some doubts about that a newly diagnosed DPDR can be rapidly fixed. It's still unknown for me how many and in how depth neurochemical effects were produced in our brains due to a long lasting generalized anxiety and whether those effects could be reversible in a short period of time.

The truth is that the recovery process is a long-distance race, a **daily effort for many months, even years** till recover normalcy of thought.

Regardless the rightness of my hypothesis to understand what DPDR consists of, more or less adjusted to the current psychological/neurological knowledge, **the fact is thanks to a time period practicing a number of concrete exercises I could get out from the mental state** I fall in April 1988 and that I was able to connect again in November 2014.

I am fully aware that everything I did to get out of this state and I can evaluate **the right hemisphere/limbic system contribution to a normal thought**. After living so many years in a dissociated brain I can determine in what degree the right hemisphere can contribute to provide **normalcy and especially peace** of mind.

Although the reasons which led us to the disconnection have already disappeared (post-traumatic stress, taking drugs/other type of meds, philosophical thoughts about the self...), **DPDR tends to stay permanently** with us as an state which alters the perception of the self and the world. It is an stable state. Hence its complete eradication is very complex.

7.2 BASIC PRINCIPLES OF THE METHOD

If you are planning to begin the re-connection process you must take into account:

1. It's a MUST that **factors which built the emotional barrier have already disappeared** and the person affected has already reached a stable living environment with the least possible number of worries which allow the relaxation of the brain zone altered by the DPDR. You should receive **psychological therapy** by a professional if you haven't assumed the emotional trauma which led you to the disconnection.

2. Individual must **accept and know the nature of his disorder and be aware that the recovery time could be very long** (months, even years). Impatience can spoil the recovery, it will bring you an additional anxiety which might interfere with the healing process. Remember that it's a long-distance race. Don't put dates on it.

3. Patient should lead a life as normal as possible most of the day and **reserve daily from half an hour to an entire hour for his recovery process**. It's counter-productive getting obsessed with doing exercises all the time. You'll get tired and will be discouraged. The thought framework change cannot be accelerated no matter how much you try to speed up the process.

4. Recovery is made basically **by yourself, in silence and in motion**. The idea is to connect with the 'mute' hemisphere, with the hemisphere of senses, of time, space and emotions.

5. It's good to follow the general guidelines to **reduce the anxiety** by any standard treatment. Remember that **although is necessary to remove anxiety to remove the DPDR, it won't be enough**. Therefore you should decrease the pace of your life and reduce responsibilities. Taking often a deep breath will be helpful to success!

6. Remember the issue consists of taking part of the world again, not to isolate from it. You must **make substantial efforts to interact with things**, with people, thinking the consequences of pushing this, climbing above that car or kicking this stone. Paradoxically you should **give due emphasis to the details you used to consider less important**: color, shapes, evaluate if you like them or not ... So it's certainly not advisable to perform any activity requiring concentration. It deals with paying attention to the whole-picture, to the surroundings, **to your own mood and the people around you**.

7.3   THE TWENTY BASIC EXERCISES

To be effective in overcoming this emotional blocking **a variety of exercises must be done systematically for at least several months**.

The idea is to combine a 'semi-normal' life suffering DPDR with the practice of exercises for half an hour to an hour per day. The challenge is fixing 'the motor in flight' without the plane falls. Life doesn't stop for anybody. You must continue living, working, studying, relating with others, going to lunches, dinners, events... despite you have decided to escape from DPDR.

From the 20 exercises, although **all of them have been designed against unreality**, there are some more suitable to treat Depersonalization and others more suitable to solve vision and perception of the world problems resulting from Derealization.

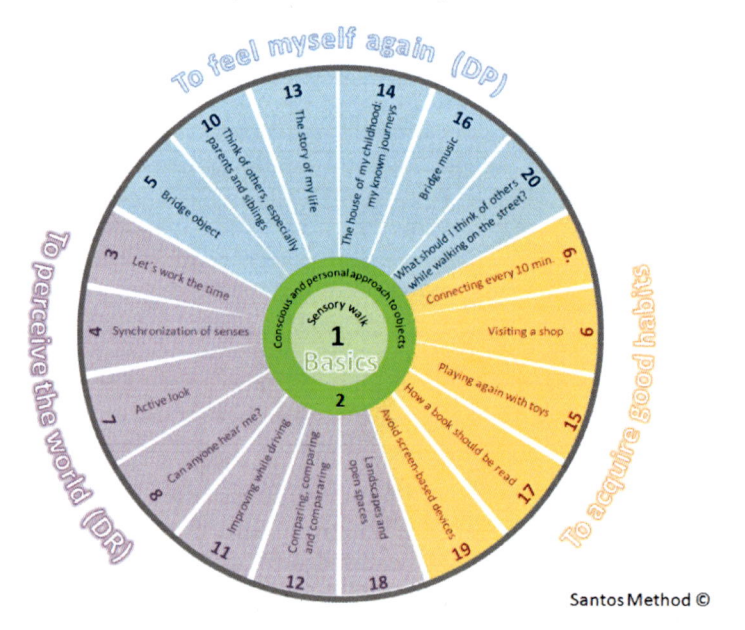

To feel myself again (DP)
To perceive the world (DR)
To acquire good habits

1. Basics — Sensory walk
2. Conscious and personal approach to objects
3. Let's work the time
4. Synchronization of senses
5. Bridge object
6. Visiting a shop
7. Active look
8. Can anyone hear me?
9. Connecting every 10 min.
10. Think of others, especially parents and siblings
11. Improving while driving
12. Comparing, comparing and comparating
13. The story of my life
14. The house of my childhood: my known journeys
15. Playing again with toys
16. Bridge music
17. How a book should be read
18. Landscapes and open spaces
19. Avoid screen-based devices
20. What should I think of others while walking on the street?

Santos Method ©

BASIC EXERCISES 1 AND 2

The central exercises of the circle were the key to begin to break the unreality wall that separated me from the world. Both two consist of walking, the first one freely and in a subsequent phase focusing on a relatively far object which is on our path, the exercise number 2.

The first one tries to free ourselves from the somatized or entrenched anxiety which causes that we do everything quickly and in an automatic way. Since **we are deprived from a concrete objective** when going outside that fact **encourage our mind can try to pay attention of all that surrounds us**.

Number 2; in addition to that, consists of having a walk in a relaxed way, trying to practice the **distance and the time** remaining to reach a determined object. Distance and time are closely related, one is not understood without the other.

These two exercises should take part of our daily recovery habit since movement and the consequences derived from our body touching real objects are strongly powerful in the process.

EXERCISES TO TREAT DEREALIZATION (3, 4, 7, 8, 11, 12 y 18)

This set of exercises have an effect especially over a right perception of the world: **recovering the meaning of hours** and the days of the week, working on the **coordinated functioning of all our senses** in order to perceive the world that surround us, **relearning to look** and observe the objects focusing on the scenario and its dimensions and shapes, **paying attention to the sound we produce** in any moment and who could be hearing us, seizing the moment when we travel by car to **perceive adequately the landscape** giving a meaning for us, **making efforts to compare** everything we perceive now with other previous perceptions to give meaning to what we feel and finally practicing the projection of our own body **imagining the**

consequences and real sensations we have thanks to be present in reality.

Basically the purpose of these exercises is **refocusing on <u>paying attention consciously</u>** to all that surround us.

EXERCISES TO TREAT DEPERSONALIZATION (5, 10, 13, 14, 16 y 20)

There are many DPDR patients specifically complaining about having lost their personality, about being uncomfortable with their identity, without knowing certainly if they are real or not, doubting about their own existence, doubting if they have really lived a previous life since the memories of personal history are unclear, lacking images and out of time. This set of exercises is designed for them, for those annoyed when thinking of themselves.

The first of them is using a bridge object, reserved to make efforts in order to **recover the feelings and the correct way of thinking when we used to touch, observe and feel a familiar object** from the days we were MYSELF, when we were OK. Another, the number 10th tries **to keep in mind all the times those people our personality was formed with**, typically in the bosom of a family, normally parents, siblings or close relatives. It applies to any person who raised us and meant so much to us. Our personality is formed from what the rest of people think about us.

Another exercise very important is' **the story of my life'**, especially for those suffering DPDR for some years consisting of put in practice the autobiographical memory probably distorted by the dissociation. Remembering, writing and placing correctly our memories on a sheet it's **extremely helpful to recover the sensation of having had a life**. Related to the latter it's remembering the places where we used to go when we were ok, remembering the paths we used to walk will be helpful to recover our lost identity. There is another exercise, the number 14th which works spatial location and relates it with the story of our life. It's called *'The house of my childhood'*.

The next exercise is "bridge music", **helpful to evoke by means of the integrating effect of music the time-spatial sensations from our time when we were ok**. The same effect is produced when we visualize movies from our childhood or adolescence when we were mentally healthy.

Finally we will work our image before the rest of people with the exercise number 20. To do this we must **remember and repeat what sets us apart from the rest**. We should make a list with our strengths and the main achievements in life and comparing ourselves with the others' life. Through this exercise we will keep in mind again that we are different from the rest and that we have our own and unique preferences. It works on **self-esteem** because there will be always something we do better than the rest.

EXERCISES TO ACQUIRE GOOD HABITS (6, 9, 15, 17 y 19)

At this point in the book you know more or less what DPDR consists of, **the inability to pay attention personally and consciously to all that surrounds us.** One of the main characteristics of DPDR is the isolation between our minds, rational and emotional. This fact makes you feel our body is detached from our reasoning. Since we tend to do everything in an automatic way, without a full control, it's convenient to **avoid some errors very frequent** in our behavior and to force us to acquire good habits which will foster our re-connection.

The practice of the five exercises of this section will force us to acquire good habits.

A frequent error is focusing on **fulfilling a task without resting enough** in order to perceive what surrounds us, even our body, our emotions, taking that into account and feel the time, etc. Hence the meaning of exercise number 6, connect every 10 minutes.

Another mistake is remaining **too focused on our objective** in life, in our duty, in what we must purchase, for instance, when we walk by a shop. So focused and anxious about what we must do that we forget relaxing and perceiving the details of the general situation, of our body, of the environment, of the image we offer to the world... Exercise nº9 reminds you **what harmful is isolating from the real world for DPDR patients by reading a book, using the headphones of a Smartphone... specially when walking** along the street or when we are within a social environment surrounding by people. Don't make it easy to the DPDR! Don't cut you off from the world! You must remain opened to the emotions and external stimuli.

It's worth mentioning the exercise number 15, which suggests us **playing as a therapy** to re-connect both hemispheres. It is vital enjoying again from interacting with a real, suggestive and colored object as a toy is. Playing with real and **physical objects** causes that the barrier between logical and emotional parts be weakened and it be finally broken. In a sense, the exit of this dissociation consists of coming back to a normal state of mind, a state **when we used to enjoy from our stuff**.

Although reading books is always highly recommended for every normal and healthy people, for a DPDR patient it's not so good because it leads the mind to maintain the detachment from the real world, recreating a fictitious one. Exercise nº17 uses books as a therapy to revert to who we were. **Books, used as bridge objects, are therapeutics.** To do this we must see books with other eyes, the emotional mind ones. Their texture and cover must be perceived, their pages must be smelled, we should notice the color of the printed ink, be aware about that book is ours or not... The key is **to perceive books again by its aspect**, not by its content. We should **avoid reading books in a compulsive way**, including new subjects, attending new courses since we will be including more rational knowledge to our left hemisphere but without solving the underlying problem with our personality. Paradoxically, **what allows us to grow rationally could obstruct us the return to normalcy**, enjoying again from perceive simple things of the real world. If you still had to read something, do it progressively doing frequent breaks.

At last, another major error and extremely widespread practiced consists of spending much of our time pending of screens, TVs, computers, tablets, smart phones, videogames, cinema projectors, ebooks... since they **isolate us from the physical and real world**. Time spent on new technologies must be controlled and limited because they generate strong addition to DPDR patients. Sharing experiences or searching information about DPDR don't solve the problem, while it is true that knowing we are not alone can alleviate the patient. **The solution to DPDR is outside, in the real world** of the senses, far from electronic devices and **near the real objects**.

Here below I will transcribe the posts where exercises were included, translated to English language and chronologically. The **20 exercises** intended to treat naturally the DPDR disorder were published in http://dpdrspain.blogspot.com in Spanish and http://dpdrenglish.blogspot.com from October 26th, 2014 to April 22nd, 2015.

EXERCISE nº1 - "Sensory walking"
Sunday, October 26th, 2014

One of the most important habits to find the way toward your recovery is to be accustomed **to go out of home to have a walk** for just half an hour every day.

Previous conditions:

1. Go **alone**. Just your mind and your body.
2. No worries. It is recommended **walking** at the end of the day, **at late afternoon**. Your only worry should be getting home to sleep.
3. **Comfortable** clothing.
4. Your unique **purpose for walking should be your recovery**. Without any errand or command.

Objective:

Get **a space and a special moment** for yourself, free of distractions and complex thoughts.

For this half an hour we **might perform much more healthy exercises** that I will describe in subsequent posts within this blog.

What must I do?

Just crossing your door you should pay attention consciously at **everything** you do, see, hear, feel,... during your walk, **just as a kid would do**.

Focus in **not thinking about transcendent or abstract ideas** such as challenges you must do tomorrow at work, at school or in your own problem of derealization.

Just **pay attention to the movement of your body**, your feet treading the cobbles of the pavement, walking on the sidewalk, looking at parked cars, trees, semaphores, the colors of the things...

Try to **enjoy** your walk!

EXERCISE nº2 -"Consciously and individual approximation to objects"
Wednesday, October 29th, 2014

At any moment of the day, and especially during our daily "sensory walking" we can practice this exercise in order to connect better with the real world. This exercise is based on several "simple" steps:

1. While you were walking, **follow with your look** a comparatively distant object you will found on the road (i.e.: a tree, a car, a mailbox ...). For a DR person, this action, apparently easy, is not simple. Ordinary people can do it unconsciously when they walk.

2. Observe **how changes** as you approximate to it. Look at it in 3 dimensions. Don't distract your look! The key is to observe.

3. Calculate **how long** takes for being able to touch it. **Think of what would happen** if YOU reach this object and push it. Is it very heavy? Could you lift it?, If you hit it hard, would you hurt yourself?, Are you taller than it?, If you jump, could you touch it?, If YOU sit down on it...what would happen?, and, If you crush it?

4. **When you reach** the object, **touch it**, go round it to watch it well, smell it... **feel it**. Tap it, hit it, hear the sound, feel the texture when you run your fingers through it...

5. **What is the link between YOU and that object?,** the color it has... Have you ever seen it at the past? When? Have you seen other objects like this before?, do you like it?, would you like to stay one for you?, Where would you put it?, What would be the reaction of your family or friends?

IT IS IMPORTANT TO FOLLOW ALL THE STEPS

Your rational mind, not affected by DP/DR, will say to you that this exercise does not make any sense. Why must I do that? It is absurd! It will say to you that you already see things ok when you are having a walk. Ignore that thought! Don't be afraid to be ridiculous if you touch something or jump to know if you can touch a branch of a tree!

You must **feel things and know again what happens when your body interacts with** them.

Kids can do that continuously without think of anything else!

Points 1 to 4 of the exercise attack derealization problem and 5 serves to mitigate the depersonalization disorder you may be suffering.

EXERCISE nº3 - "Let's work the time"
Thursday, November 6th, 2014

DP/DR disorder triggers **an alteration of the perception related with passing time**, in several ways:

- Being unable to calculate properly the time elapsed between two different events.
- The clock's hours and the days of the week have ceased to mean a special relevance for us. We don't mind at what time and day we make things.
- ...

Why does this happen?

We have lost the temporal references from the past. Everybody, since childhood, has been learning to feel the pass of the time. For example we learnt to feel how long is one hour, or 5 minutes in function of the number of things that may happen in that passage of time, watching different events from the real world. **To feel the pass of the time appropriately, we have to perceive the reality that surround us thoroughly.**

If we are not fully connected to reality, the sense of the pass of the time stays distorted. We don't have anything to compare to, **there are not references.**

Another collateral effect of DP consist of **having also lost the references about which things we did at what hour of the day** before the attack of DP/DR. If one cannot connect with the things one did and thought of at certain hours of the day it is impossible that they now mean anything. **The schedule and habits we followed were part from our personality.**

PROPOSED EXERCISE nº3:

Every time you observe a watch to know the time it is, make a **conscious effort** to remember **what you used to do at this time of the day when you were ok**, what you were doing, for example, when you were a student and go walking from school to home.

Remember the entering and dismissal time, how long did it take walking from home to school?

For instance, what happened on Saturdays at 2 p.m.? What did you usually do? Where did you use to go? Whom did you go with? What did you do different on Sunday mornings respect to the rest of the days of the week? Till what time did you stay up late? And what was the last time permitted to arrive home?

Access to those temporal memories activates the memory of your FORMER EGO, of YOUR CUSTOMS, HABITS, TIMETABLES... So it will help you to improve in your depersonalization.

EXERCISE nº4 - "Synchronization of senses"
Tuesday, November 11th, 2014

Ordinary people not affected by DP/DR use his five senses synchronously to discern the world:

*When they enter a cathedral for the very first time, in a natural way, they observe the spectacular and **coloured** showcases in the windows, hear the **echo** from distant sounds, feel with their touch the reigning **cold** and **moisture**, as well as the texture of the columns, they smell the **old wood** from the benches and the odor of mold that emanates from the crypts.*

*When they make a manual activity, as typing on the keyboard, **they look at their fingers**, the keys they are pressing and **hear** the sound produced by them, **feel the texture** of them, etc...*

*When there is a conversation on the table, they **intuitively turn their head to observe** and pay attention to their tablemates.*

In a permanent state of stress or alteration by a DP/DR disorder, we can't pay attention to those details. We apparently hear well, see ok, but not as a whole, not the two senses together. That fact contributes to that our reality perception is not correct.

We indeed "see "and "hear" instead of "observe" and "listen" in a synchronized way.

Ok. We must work in that point...

EXERCISE nº4: "Synchronization of our senses":

This exercise is too simple and can be fulfill while we have our daily half an hour "sensory walk":

Exercise 4.1: "Turn your gaze mindfully to the sounds you can hear"

*Pay close attention to the sounds that surrounds you, to the conversations of people, to your footsteps and **determine / observe whence the sound comes**, It is not enough with hearing it, you should move as you get closer to the noisy source determining the position or place whence it comes.*

Exercise 4.2: "Listen mindfully the sound produced by the objects you knock"

*Produce sounds with your fingers, with your hands, with some object hitting another one, etcetera while you observe yourself doing it. It is crucial to **look at the precise point where you are touching** because it is the same place where the sound will be generated.*

EXERCISE nº5 - "Using a bridge object"
Friday, November 14th, 2014

Search in your house **an object like a book, a game, a pen, a pack of cards,** etc ... you used **before falling into depersonalization** , for which you know you spent enough time in the past, that must mean something for you (possibly it was **one of your favorites)** and is associated with moments of leisure, good times, a vacation, relax ...
The exercise involves **concentrating all your attention aware** that object, with your <u>five senses</u> and especially **try to travel to the past** and **to feel the same as you felt when you had that object in your hands**.

FEEL THAT YOU ARE THE SAME PERSON!!

Try to think who was around you when you were using that object, what did you usually think at that time? How did you use it? In essence try to connect with your former YOURSELF. How did you get it?, did you buy it or was a present?, What **did you think <u>the first time</u>** you used it ?, Whom were you with ?, Did you like using it ?, Why were you attracted by that object? , How long did you spend on it? Where was it placed before? Etcetera.

☐

You can repeat this exercise with every object that have meant something good to you in the past.

Our mind has been blocked by a permanent stress, anxiety, a wrong way of perceiving reality, a way of thinking that is not adequate. **It is therefore essential to retake the thoughts and previous concerns to connect with our TRUE OURSELF.**

EXERCISE nº6 - "Connecting every 10 minutes"
Friday, November 21st, 2014

It is normal having to deal with daily **tasks that need our concentration and abstraction from the real world**:

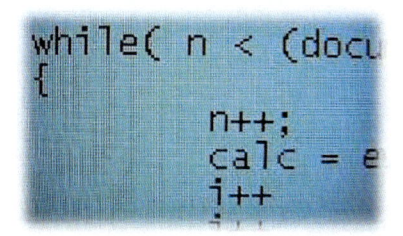

- Read or study **books**, articles, web pages on the Internet ...
- View **movies**, or listen to **music** with headphones.
- Playing **video games** (on PCs, tablets, smart phones...)
- **Programming** a computer
- Thinking for a long time in a **work or family problem that concerns us.**

And so on...

These activities naturally evade us from the real world. <u>**While we develop these activities we cease to pay attention to what surrounds us**</u> creating a propitious environment to the occurrence of derealization disorders.

This evasion of the real world, combined with other factors such as stress , work pressure, trauma, anxiety ... If it lasts for a long time can be the trigger for an episode of DP / DR.

In the exercise I propose today we will attack the excess concentration of our mind immersed in one of these risk activities:

Exercise No. 6: "Connecting every 10 minutes"

*If we're watching a **movie** at home at night, keep a light that illuminates the room to, and for about 10 minutes long, stop paying attention to the movie and: focus on objects within reach, look our legs, our hand, arms, be aware of our position (if we are sitting, lying, comfortable or not, ...), look at the other people who might be watching the same movie, etc...*

*If we are required to **read or study printed material** , either on paper on a computer screen, do the same, stop approximately every 10 minutes to connect with the objects, place, our own body and people that surround us. You don't need to get up, but you MUST stop reading the book, move your head to every direction focusing and connecting with the environment.*

Avoid software and addictive games. If you must face to one, stop every few minutes to acquire information from the space where your body is located.

Do you have a profession or hobby that requires you concentrating for long periods of time?

BE CAREFUL AND TAKE THESE MEASURES!!

EXERCISE nº7 - "Active look"
Friday, November 28th, 2014

In this post we will raise awareness about how important it is *to change* **the way we watch the things** around us. A necessary change towards normalcy :-)

A style of "**ACTIVE LOOK**" is to **be constantly focusing different objects at different distances to be aware of everything around us**. Exactly <u>THE OPPOSITE TO BE CONCENTRATED</u>, <u>ABSORTED</u> in our thoughts, far from reality.

Vision with DPDR   Focusing

On the left you can see the confused (in fact, it is not blurry as is represented here) image a DP / DR person perceives. However if you ask him about what he can see he will say correctly that there is a bottle, some fruits and a doll, but meaning nothing personal to him / her. **No memories evoked or emotional /temporal/spatial implications**.

On the right side of the picture a healthy person observes and processes the image. His gaze is focused on the details, evaluating 3D images, people related with that objects and wondering about their meaning.
Typical questions arisen: Who left this here ?, my mother?, my wife?, I love bananas, might I take one ?, is it time to eat something ?, should collect all that objects and put them in its correct place ?, Who has taken away that stuffed and why?, are they near the edge of the table ?, etc ...

ALL the objects around us, including our own body SHOULD mean something to us. A normal person **unconsciously processes the next items when he observes a REAL object:**

- Is it mine or not? Whose is it?
- How far is from MY BODY? Can I take it without moving or have to get up? How?
- Is it the first time I can see something like that? If not, which are the differences respect to others I've seen before?
- Is it heavy or light? If I lift it ... will it weigh a lot?
- Is it nice to see? Do I like it?, is it special for ME ?, does it have attractive colors?
- How long is there? Who put it there?

At the same time we must **be aware of our body** , we have to look our <u>hands</u>, <u>fingers</u>, <u>arms</u>, <u>legs</u>, <u>feet</u>, in essence what we manage to see from our <u>chest</u> and TO OBSERVE their features and possible changes in them. Is my hair longer? Have I got new moles?, are my joints hurting me anywhere?

WE MUST PERCEIVE OUR BODY!

We must pay attention to **the position of our body when we sit** or when we stand, if we are comfortable or not, when an object touches us and bother us. We must also pay attention **in how we dress,** what we are wearing, what shoes, what sweaters or sweatshirts, what pants, do I keep the ones I like ?, When did I buy them ?, I went shopping with someone to buy it or someone gave me as a present ?, **When and where?**, on what occasion?

It is also essential **to locate our body** in the place where we are:
Are we near a wall? Is this room equal to other room I had known somewhere before, is it a street that is reminiscent of another of my childhood? ...

EXERCISE nº8 - "Can anybody hear me?"
Sunday, November 30th, 2014

Let me a break, I'll make a survey among my readers.
*Is your sense of hearing working ok? Since you have DP/DR are you **feeling that something is wrong hearing sounds**? Have you done a medical hearing test and yet everything is okay...? It is strange, isn't it?*

Would you mind to write a comment *on this post to tell me how your perception of sounds is, what happens when you talk to someone, what do you feel? ... As the title of this exercise says: Can anybody hear me? :-)*

I propose this simple exercise related to the perception of hearing:

EXERCISE nº8 - *Can anybody hear me?*
Make a **sound with your fingers, give a slap, talk to someone, yell your name, whisper, click your tongue, clears your throat, etc ... ...** let's experience sounds coming out of you. Try different sound intensities from the lowest to the highest and observe the reactions of others, <u>look their faces to perceive their emotions, to feel you are in this real world and can affect others.</u>

Pay attention and ask yourself:

1. Sounds are high or low? Medium? Try to speak very softly.
2. Which is the level of the sound **people is listening to me?** i.e.: my brother, my mother, my roommate or work fellow from home or the office?
3. When I go down to the street *i.e.: In my sensory daily walk, ¿* **who may be listening me if I speak, shout or sing a song**? Move your head slightly from left to right, searching for people who might hear you.

As you can notice, to answer these questions adequately is necessary also use the vision(remember the Exercise 4 - synchronization of the senses) turning your head from left to right **to detect the direction of the sound**.

A person with DP / DR does not pay adequate attention to the volume of his voice, or the sounds is transmitting... just pay attention to the content . We could say that he takes into account just the pure and simple message and NOT THE FORM OR DIRECTION IN WHICH THE SOUND IS GENERATED, NOR THE EMOTIONS CONTAINED IN THE VOICE.

In order to return to be placed properly in the real world is extremely important to recover this sensitivity **THINKING OF (IMAGINE) THE WAY OTHERS PERCEIVE US WHEN WE SPEAK.**

EXERCISE nº9 - "Visiting a shop"
Thursday, December 4th, 2014

One of the reasons that led us to the DP / DR was being **so concerned about an issue**, **so focused on something or so traumatized by an experience** that our mind decided to protect and insulate us from the reality around our body.

Somehow, the logical mind **remains *unplugged*** from those negative emotions which arose when we had to do something, probably against our will.

Example: In my case my obsession was to study as much as possible to pass exams of my engineering career. Everywhere I went in my leisure time, vacations, etcetera my mind was always concerned for the exams. In that way I couldn't pay adequate attention to my environment, we could say that I didn't care at all. I was just calm only when I was studying. There was a continual contradiction between my body and my mind, which ended abruptly in a severe episode of derealization.

Can you live without paying attention to what surrounds your body?

Undoubtedly yes, it is precisely what happens with DP / DR dissociation. Your body goes on "autopilot" for life while you are worried about your obsession. At first it can be controlled at will, after the "stroke", it becomes permanent.

EXERCISE # 9 - "Visiting a shop"

For example, when you go to a counter of a shop or a store to buy or order something and have to wait in a queue:

- **Look around** to see if you are annoying somebody. Watch your feet and place them correctly.
- **Compare your height** with those of other people you have around. Are you higher or lower?
- **Compare your age** roughly with them. What age would you say they are?
- **Calculate how far** is your body from the walls of the room, the door, the window, the counter, ...
- **Look closely** everything there on the counter, even things you are not intended to buy. The idea is <u>not only to</u> <u>focus on what you need to do</u> on the shop: what else do they sell? What type of cash register / POS they have, read the name of the clerk on his shirt.
- **Account**, including you, how many people are in the queue. Do you know in what order you go in the line?
- Do you feel **hot or cold**? Are you comfortable? ...
- **What's that smell**? Have you ever smelled that scent? Where before?

- What **sounds** are in the trade? Is there any radio on? Are the other people in the queue talking or are they silent? Why don't you talk to someone in the queue?

IF YOU WANT TO RECOVER THE NORMALITY...

... STOP AVOIDING THE SITUATION USING YOUR SMARTPHONE, READING A NEWSPAPER, LISTENING MUSIC <u>OR THINKING ABOUT WORRIES FROM THE PAST OR THE FUTURE IN OTHER PLACE DIFFERENT FROM WHERE YOU ARE RIGHT NOW!</u>

In short, you must **be alert to the real world** , <u>you should certainly focus your eyes to what is around you</u> (Exercise 7: An Active Seeing) and <u>make an effort to feel the pace of time.</u>

You should be awake, AT PRESENT TIME!!

EXERCISE nº10 - "Keep in mind others, specially parents and siblings"
Tuesday, December 9th, 2014

Did you know that one of the keys to get over our DP / DR is **consider what others, especially close relatives or friends, think of us**?

Everything we are, **our personality, has been forged slowly through relationships with others**, **especially** those most influential like **father, mother and siblings** (I mean those who have educated us and the rest of the people have lived with us during our childhood and youth)

☐

Our **habits** at home, the **time of the day** you used to eat, when they used to go to bed, what they usually did at home on Sunday, etc ... everything is governed by our relationship with them. In a house it is known naturally what is normal and what is not, **what is right and what is wrong**. There is a **vital history and shared values** . Like it or not, they ARE OUR REFERENCE BASE.

Take them into account IS IMPORTANT!

EXERCISE #10: "Take into account people who raise you specially parents and siblings"

(This exercise can be done even if you are not in touch with your

family. Just go back in time, remember and imagine you're still living there, at your parents')

Ask specific questions about the members of your family you grew up:

- Would you like the work that I have or what I am studying?
- Where is my brother now? When was the last time I saw him ?, And the last time I called him on the phone?
- If my mother were here in my room or in my current house ... What would be her opinion about what she could see? And my father and my brothers?
- What games did we play together?
- Where were we going at holidays ?, What did we use to do?, Where did we use to go ?, What was my favorite game at that time ?, What about theirs?
- What music did you like the most?
- What was the hobby of each member of my family? What did they like?
- How much money was your week's pay? What did you spend that on?...

This exercise primarily fights against **depersonalization**. If you notice something in your mind shudders when wondering these questions ... OK. EVERYTHING IS FINE!

EXERCISE №11 - "Getting better while driving"
Monday, December 22nd, 2014

A person with DP / DR can get the driver's license and driving perfectly. I attest that, because I did, and many other complex tasks.

In our state, the <u>natural tendency is to focus on the road</u>, driving, and look ahead continuously. How to improve our DP / DR is based on the following exercises:

1. **Slow down, to one speed that is more comfortable** to look at anything other than just the road. 90 km/h is fine. In addition, we reduce stress and accumulated tension.
2. Think about where you are now. **How far are you** from where you lived when you were okay? Is it very far? Which way, **which way would you go to your old house**?, How would you do to get there if you had to walk ?, When would you reach a known point by which you went through many times when you were okay?

3. Have you ever been on other occasions in this place? When? Who were you with?
4. Pay attention to the bridges crossing the road. Are they too far up from the ground? How far? **What would happen** if you crash with one of the bridge pillars? ... Phew!! Observe the vegetation, the median and the buildings surrounding the road.

5. Notice **other cars** left and right of your lane, look at the color and model. Watch its occupant. Is it older than you? Could it be an old classmate? Which could be his occupation now? Do you like his/her car? **Imagine it is a car toy,** like those you played with when you were a kid. **Imagine you could handle it and could move it back and forth.**

Of course, <u>keep looking at the road frequently to prevent an accident, but try TO FOCUS AND MOVE ACTIVELY YOUR EYES LEFT AND RIGHT TO OBSERVE THE LANDSCAPES AND OTHER OBJECTS</u> both outside and inside the car.

EXERCISE nº12 - "Comparing, comparing and comparing again"
Sunday, December 28th, 2014

By now, we know that our DP / DR dissociation likely comes from a **weak communication between two areas** or brain functions, one related to our body, time and space and the other, related to words, our consciousness and abstract concepts.

Although both still perform their functions, our **unpleasant feeling** comes from the fact that **our rational, logic mind** does not have easy access to the other part and therefore **cannot control the space-time of our life time or adequately perceive the world** around us. Even knowing that it doesn't mean any sense, we distinguish two parts within us , we feel as spectators of our own body. That fact may cause a panic attack in some individuals.

For example: a normal mind without DP / DR, is able to stop their own logical thoughts for a moment and looking consciously in a special way (check nº7 exercise, active look) to any ordinary object controlling the following information "not logical" that comes from the "other side":

- *What time can be according to the intensity and angle of light I can see out the window?*
- *How big is this room compared to the home where I lived before?*
- *How long has passed since I've seen last, eg, my brother?*
- *When did I have a glance to this book?*
- *What do I want to do now?*
- *What I'm doing now; is it appropriate to ME, to MY PERSONALITY?*
- *What did I do yesterday? And the last week? What would I do differently this week?*
- *What am I planning to do tomorrow?*
- *How long that I do not wear these shoes?*
- *Do I love my wife or my husband, girlfriend / boyfriend? What will I tell them when I meet him/her?*
- *Where have I seen this before? Are these floor tiles like parent's house?*
- *Etcetera.*

There are a few **types of questions that can help us a lot** to reconstruct the puzzle as **answers NO LOGIC, NOT ABLE TO BE reasoned**, the right answers are in the "other side". If we don't want to give a random answer, deny the question or avoid the situation, WE SHOULD ACCESS to that part of our brain we want to connect to.

Excellent exercise!

EXERCISE nº12 - Compare SPECIFIC objects!
Located in your living room, **watch the main table**. As it is not be the first table you've seen in your life, ask yourself the following questions:

- <u>When was the first time</u> you saw this table? Did you go to the furniture store to buy it? Before this one was there another? Which one do you prefer?
- <u>How is it compared to the table in your room</u>?, Is it highest? Is it made in wooden or metal? What color is one and the other?, Which of them is heavier?, Which is wider? Stretch out your hands and feel its dimensions.
- <u>Answer the same questions respect to your work desk or table where you study in school</u>, college or university.
- Stand in front of it and see how high is it compared to your legs? Sit on each chair around the table and think where you'd be more comfortable to write with a pen?

Notice **the layout of the room**, where are the armchairs, where is it the TV? Where are the chairs, and the bookstores?

Do you like the current layout more than the old one? Where did you use to sit at this time?

COMPARE ALL YOU CAN SEE: places, objects, heights, widths, dimensions respect to LONG AGO WHEN YOU WERE RIGHT!

santos.barrioscanseco@gmail.com

EXERCISE Nº13 - "The story of my life"
Tuesday, December 30th, 2014

Today I propose a very useful exercise to fight against this monster called DEPERSONALIZATION.

EXERCISE nº13: - "The story of my life"

1. Take a **sheet of paper**, standard size A4 or better the larger A3 (it depends of the number of months/years you have been suffering DP/DR)

2. Place it landscape and write at the upper left corner **the previous year** to the year you suffered the DP stroke. In my case, 1987.

3. Below, at 2 cm approx., write the next year, the year of your disorder (in my case 1988) and so on until reaching the current year (2014 now). You can turn the sheet if necessary to the other side.

4. At the upper side of the sheet and close to the right of the first year you will write place the labels corresponding to the twelve months of the year, from JAN to DEC.

5. Draw parallel lines, horizontals to separate clearly each year and verticals to separate months or quarters if you prefer.

6. FILL IN THE STORY OF YOUR LIFE: Place in the calendar, approximately, when **the most significant events of your life** happened during those months, quarters, years:

    o   When you started a **new job or project** and when you finished it.
    o   When you **fell in love** and when this **relationship was over**.
    o   When you suffered your disconnection **DP/DR**
    o   **When** and **where** you had your **vacations** (summer, winter, ...)
    o   When you passed your **driving license** exam.
    o   When you finished your **studies, university**... Fill in the ordinal of the courses. I mean, when you began 1st, 2nd, 3rd, etc...
    o   When you **passed that exam so important** for you
    o   When you **moved to a new house, a new city, a new country**
    o   When you or your relatives suffered an **important accident or trauma**, relevant in your life.
    o   When **your kids be borne** (if you have any), otherwise **nephews** or friend's children.
    o   **Wedding dates** you attended, even yours, ☺
    o   **Travels** you made to especial places, and so on...

It would be better using **colors** and putting **your age** besides every year of the calendar.

MAKE THIS EFFORT TO LOOK BACK AT YOUR PAST AND SOLVE THE PUZZLE!

WHEN
WHERE
WHAT WORRIED TO ME, <u>SPECIALLY THE FIRST YEAR AND MONTHS BEFORE MY DP/DR STROKE</u>

(c) santos.barrioscanseco@gmail.com

EXERCISE nº14 – The house of my childhood - "My known paths"
Friday, 2 de January de 2015

One of the reasons to feel **confused and disoriented** when we go down the street with DP / DR is that **we are not comparing** the path we are following NOW with the well known paths we followed when we were kids and **we were living in our parents'**

THOSE DAYS WHEN WE WERE OK!
GO BACK TO THE PAST TO <u>FEEL</u> HOW WAS LEAVING HOME!

Everyone gradually learned to go to unknown sites. There was a first time we were allowed to **throw the trash in the container**, one time in which we were allowed **to go to buy a loaf of bread** at a nearby store. Then **we started going alone to school** for a slightly longer route, we learned to go through many roads, streets, each one with its attractions and feelings.

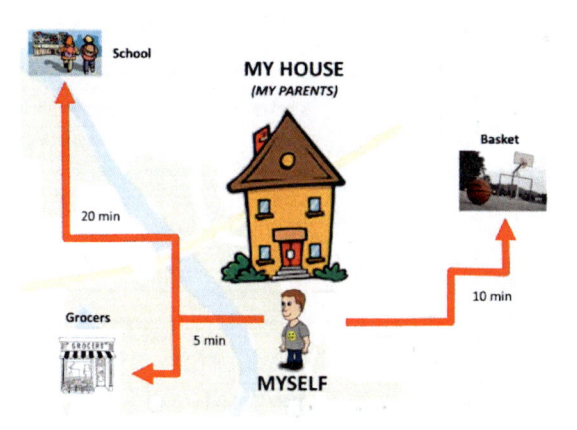

We learned **the time it took us to get to school** and not being late. That distance and that time is one of our basic references, even NOW, no matter the years have passed.

Some days, our parents, grandparents, uncle, aunt... took us by subway or bus **to some unknown and further place**. What a **thrill**! We were providing all our attention! Can you remember?

Especially, **the first time**

There was always a first time for everything!

Moreover we were **storing a time history of these possible routes** to get to different places. As well as potential **hazards or good things** from each of these routes. Now we don't have a good access to that memory. We must practice actively the access to it...

EXERCISE No. 14: "THE HOUSE OF MY CHILDHOOD - My known paths"

Close your eyes for a moment while sitting on a sofa and ***imagine you are in the past, at your parents' house, e.g. 15 years old, more or less***. You are still ok, normal. Ask yourself these questions:

IT IS HARD, I KNOW, BUT YOU MUST TRY IT!

- What time is it now?, What day is it ?, Is it week end day or working day?, **supposing that I am with my parents at home** ... What could be doing right now?, Should I be playing?, Having a walk?, at school? ...
- How long would I have to wait to get out for a walk? Did I need permission from my parents?
- Out where did I usually go?, What were **my favorite paths**?, What were my preferences?, Going to see my friend who lived two blocks away?, Did we stay at some particular spot, maybe a shopping mall? ...

Imagine it's time to go to school ... you are going out. Where would you go? What direction would you take?

HOW DO YOU FEEL?

EXERCISE Nº15 - "Playing again with toys and dolls"
Thursday, January 8th, 2015

One of the activities that helped our brain to mature and grow healthy was PLAYING with TOYS. Playing **with toys** was very important in our childhood and we must practice again if we wish to return to a normal state:

1. **Find a toy** (little car, plane, doll ...) from your childhood or a current one very similar to those which you had before. If you have children, you can borrow one from them or mounting a new one from an egg kinder that always contains small and manageable toys.

2. Take it, look at it, feel its weight, observe its colors and looks how you MOVE IT WITH YOUR HAND as a child would play. If it is a **doll**, sit her on the couch, gather her hair in a ponytail, move it back and forth... If you have a **little car** as well, move it, park it, **simulates going down the street on your desk, at home or at your office.**

3. Do not be ashamed of it, **it is ABSOLUTELY necessary for communicate properly both brain hemispheres** between each other and recover some of the lost sensitivity. It's part of your **therapy** to overcome this.

4. When you are absorbed in your work or your studies, keep that toy close to you, look at it frequently, and play a little with him, and **make the effort to FEEL the same as felt before when you played with him years ago.**

Visit this link and check out why it is so necessary!

[The importance of playing in children](www.education.com)
(www.education.com)

santos.barrioscanseco@gmail.com

EXERCISE nº16 - "Bridge music"
Monday, January 12th, 2015

We all remember what kind of music we liked listen to before suffering our derealization. **What singer or group album should be relevant or important for us**? (Although maybe we cannot feel anything about it, for sure we can still remember its name).

EXERCISE nº16: "Music as a bridge"

Search within your memory the name of the disks or CDs you heard **one year or months before** suffering the DP / DR and **find them on youtube.com** or **spotify.com** to redisplay the cover and listen to their songs.

ORIGINAL MOTION PICTURE SOUNDTRACK
JUST CALLED TO SAY I LOVE YOU/STEVIE WONDER • LOVE LIGHT IN FLIGHT/STEVIE WONDER
IT'S YOU/DIONNE WARWICK & STEVIE WONDER • THE WOMAN IN RED/STEVIE WONDER
MOMENTS AREN'T MOMENTS/DIONNE WARWICK • WEAKNESS/DIONNE WARWICK & STEVIE
WONDER • DON'T DRIVE DRUNK/STEVIE WONDER • IT'S MORE THAN YOU

The Woman in Red

▶ Reproducir álbum

MUSIC PRODUCED BY STEVIE WONDER

8 canciones

1	The Woman In Red	4:42
2	It's You	4:56
3	It's More Than You	3:16
4	I Just Called To Say I Love You	4:44
5	Love Light In Flight	6:55
6	Moments Aren't Moments	4:33
7	Weakness	4:14
8	Don't Drive Drunk	6:36

While you are doing so **THINK YOU ARE THE SAME PERSON AS BEFORE.**

- Find out inside yourself and think **what you were doing when** you were listening to it, what time of your life you were in (school, college, work, holidays, ...) and **who was with you** at that time, whether it was summer or winter, **where** did you use to listen to it (in your room, in your car, on a mobile player while you were giving a ride, ...)

- At the same time **look at your hands or a "bridge object"** to facilitate the exercise. Your hands are the same who manipulated your tape player, CD / DVD / iPod / Mp3 than before. YOU ARE THE SAME AND SHOULD FEEL THE SAME.

- **What buttons did you have to push** to listen to this music? What color were they?, Which shape did they have? Squared, rounded? ...

ALL THIS INFORMATION IS NOT LOGIC – IT IS SPACE-TIME RELATED

VISUALIZE THE PLACE WHERE YOU USED TO LISTEN TO THAT ALBUM AND FEEL YOURSELF THERE AGAIN!

santos.barrioscanseco@gmail.com

EXERCISE nº17 - "Reading books?"
Friday, January 16th, 2015

While we have DP/DR we **should not read too many books unless it be imperative** in order to maintain a normal life until getting a full recovery (to be graduate, to keep our job, etc ...) and **if we must do it, do it always following the recommendation about stopping at least every ten minutes** to connect to everything around us, even with the book itself, with its cover, leaves,...

And preferably real books, tangible, with sheets of paper, **not digital**. Electronic books, unless they are "scanned originals", cannot evoke memories that interest us.

And why is not recommended while we are suffering DP/DR? This is because although **the content of a book may evoke real items, it cannot substitute real things that surround us. It is another way of escaping from OUR CURRENT REALITY and delay the cure.**

Our exercise is based on **seeing the book as a real object**, *not as a content to be devoured in a linear and not stop way until it is finished.*

EXERCISE º17 - "a different use of books as therapy"

At home there are two types of books. Those who you read BEFORE catching DP/DR and those acquired LATER.

There are YOUR BOOKS and others that are not. The distinction is important because we want to recover OURSELF, OUR PERSONALITY.

*Preferably you should use the books from **BEFORE**, as they will connect with the past, and those that are **YOURS**.*

- *Look through the shelves at those books that are **yours and prior to the dp/dr** stroke. Focus first on them.*
- ***Take one of them**, feel their **weight**, open their pages, touch the **texture** of their leaves and **smell** inside. Look carefully at the **front** and **back** page.*

- *Ask yourself the following questions with the book in your hands:*

- **When** did I buy it? **Why** did I buy it? **Where** did I buy it? Could I read it completely? Where did I use to read it? What worried me at that moment?
- Is it bounded with transparent plastic?, when did I put that cover? How it got this shelf? Has it always been here? Where was it when I was okay?
- Who saw me reading it? Family? Friends? Classmates or work colleagues?
- What would happen if I throw it to the floor? Would it make a loud sound?
- If it is a textbook, did I work on every chapter?
- Have it got handwriting notes from my own in the margins? Does it appear any date?
- Think meanwhile you are touching it... I AM THE SAME "ME" THAT TOUCH IT TIME AGO, and do a carefully observation again.

Do not read it at this point! Just **passed to another book** and repeat the former steps.

That is, we must review the books superficially, having a look at their physical characteristics and memories that could evoke to us.

BUT NOT THE CONTENT ITSELF!!

santos.barrioscanseco@gmail.com

EXERCISE Nº18 - "Managing landscapes and open spaces"
Sunday, January 25th, 2015

Does the vision of a landscape confuse you? And what do you think of the diffused light in cloudy days. Does it increase the numbness feeling and increases the typical "blurry" vision of derealization? (Rather than blurred, we should say imperfect or incomplete)

You wonder 'and what must I do with a landscape? What should I think about it?' It's really hard for me noticing something concrete. It is a little torture, isn't?

EXERCISE # 18 - "Landscapes and open spaces"

We reach the street and we face a landscape outdoors. What to do?

Firstly to **"understand and manage" the brightness of the sky and of the objects** that we can see we should look at the **time** it is (i.e. 13:40). We should also notice **the height and position of the sun** above the horizon and fight to remind us of <u>what we were doing at this time when we were fine</u> (months or years ago). It works wonderfully for me remember my school days when I was under a strict routine and schedules. *For example, at 13:40 I know that I was out from school at 13:30 and it took me 10 minutes go down the avenue called 'Barcelona City'. I know that at that time was a bit hungry and when I got home about 14:00 my mother would be preparing the meal.* WE HAVE to rediscover THE MEANING OF HOURS OF THE DAY.

Every time of the day should evoke memories and feelings of the past

It is also important to think about what is/was the **season** of the year. I know this fact can evoke different sensations. The brightness depending on the hour and the season is quite different and characteristic. For example, in winter shadows are longer and the days much shorter than in summer. Our right hemisphere has been always capturing these nuances. Unable to access it, this kind of details are confusing for us.

Projecting our body:
If we can see a billboard we must imagine for a moment that we are touching its metal holder. We can also imagine that we are sitting on top of the sign. It also serves mental manipulation. Imagine we could catch it with our hands and take it to another site. For example: Leave it on the roof of a house.

Do you know how we perceive the size of the things we see?

We must project our body upon the objects you can see in the scene

We can compare the object with our own height, with our body. Imagining that we start to scale it or embrace it. We also should mentally manipulate the cars parked and take them as if they were toy cars. **Our body has to participate in the real things! and OUR BODY IS THE MEASURE OF ALL THINGS!**

Thinking about it (mental manipulation) has equal or even more therapeutic effect than doing it (action performed)

    For any questions, you know, send me an email
                                  :-)

    santos.barrioscanseco@gmail.com

EXERCISE nº19 - "Avoiding screen-based devices"
Wednesday, February 4th, 2015

The information technologies you are using in this moment may bring you good things and bad things**:**

Good things: the contribution of instant information among different people scattered across the globe, e.g the dpdrenglish blog, Facebook messenger, whatsapp...

Bad things: addiction, incapability of disconnecting from the virtual world, abstraction and conscious avoidance of the real world

In our state, as a general rule **it is not appropriate to visualize 2D screens from ebooks / smart phones, tablets, PCs, TVs, etc...**

Exercise nº19 - "Disengaging from 2D screens"

Have you ever heard about "phubbing"?

- **Do not use the smart phone / tablet while you're eating**. You should pay attention to your surroundings, to the food you are taking, do not isolate yourself from the real world. You should not read a newspaper or a book. It produces the same effect.
- **Do not use your smart phone or read anything on foot**. Apart from the obvious risks (stumble, being robbed your smart phone ...) is not healthy or naturally escaping from the stimuli of the real world in any case.
- **Do not use them in dates or meetings** with peers and real friends.
- **Establish a time limit** about using screens (i.e.: 2h maximum daily). It is addictive and you know it.

The best 3D and High Definition (HD) screen

IT IS OBSERVING THE REAL WORLD

NO SCREEN CAN REPLACE IT!

SANTOS.BARRIOSCANSECO@GMAIL.COM

EXERCISE nº20 - "What should I think of others while walking on the street?"

One of the symptoms of DPDR consists of **appearing invisible** for the rest of the people.

When we are walking in the street we usually avoid looking at the rest of the people because WE DON'T EVEN KNOW WHAT TO THINK ABOUT THEM, in fact, we are not sure about their existence. They mean nothing for us. Why does this happen?

As I don't know who I am and I am not able to remember clearly what have I done in my former life due to DPDR, it seems very difficult to guess in which way the rest will react when they see me. We have lost our roots, our references and our own image. **Our image depends on what the others think about us.**

In order to remove that invisibility and recover our place again in the real world you could practice this exercise:

EXERCISE 20 - "What must I think about people when walking in the street?"

Before facing the people in the street we should **remember aspects that are unique to us**
1st - How old am I?

2nd - What were my main achievements in life?

3rd - What were my most relevant hobbies/skills? I should overpass everybody in those skills and feel proud.

4rd - Pay attention to your physical aspect. Am I well dressed?, Do I look handsome today?

... etc

Any time you face people and don't know what to think about them, you should think:

- Could it **be dangerous** crossing his/her way? Should I be frightened?
- Is he/she **physically neat, clean**? or Should I feel disgusted?
- Is he/she a **normal person** or is he/she facing **any disability**?
- Is he/she going to ask me anything? Which could it be? Could I be robbed by him/her? Could I be taken by surprise?
- Is he/she older than me, the same age or on the contrary I am older than he/she?
- If we are of the same age, **would I like to accept him/her in my own gang or group**? I didn't like every classmate of my school. I had my reasons. Can I remember why?
- If I am older, I should know more than him/her and be superior somehow. I could teach him/her things and be compassionate with him. If I don't pay attention I could hurt him/her.
- If I am younger, that person probably knows more about life than me. I should show respect and learn from his/her.
- His/her level of studies... Are lower or higher than my own level? Would he/she overpass ME?

- I was very good playing or practising my hobby. **Could he/she be better than me? Could he/she even know how to do it?** Probably not If my skill is high.
- Am I **stronger** than that person? **Taller**? More corpulent? If we had to fight... **might I win**? If I hit him/her, what would happen? (Considering physical contact helps a lot to overcome DP)l
- Is he/she more beautiful or attractive than me? Do I like him/her?
- ...

Previously, when you were alright, you wondered those questions automatically, just within milliseconds. Now you cannot consider that info about people easily.

SO, YOU SHOULD BE MORE TRIVIAL AND TAKE CARE ABOUT APPEARANCES!

WITHOUT BEING SURE!

WITH NO LOGIC AT ALL!

ALL HEALTHY PERSON TAKE ALWAYS INTO ACCOUNT HIS/HER IMAGE AND COMPARES IT ALL THE TIME WITH OTHERS' IMAGES

santos.barrioscanseco@gmail.com

7.4 HOW IS THE RECOVERY PROCESS?

Recovery process **is slow** because we must reestablish patiently a normal pattern of thinking by practicing the exercises. If the blue semicircle represents our rational mind, the left hemisphere, and the red semicircle our emotional mind, the right hemisphere, we can graphically represent the process in the next scheme. It shows how, step by step, we should **break the emotional deadlock** of our mind.

The effects of doing the exercises of this blog can be shown in the following graph:

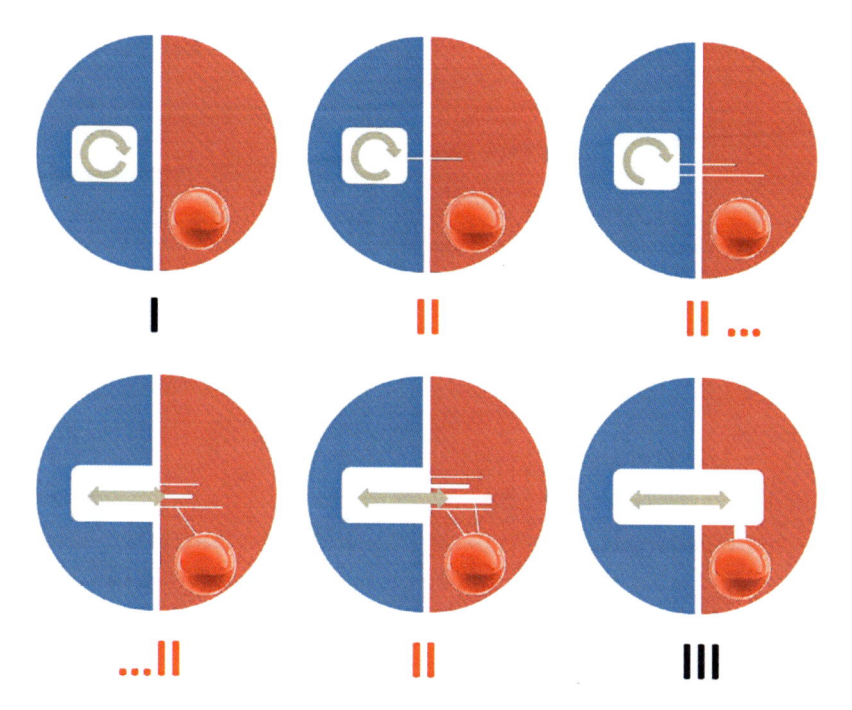

I	**II**	**II ...**
...II	**II**	**III**

We distinguish three distinct phases in the recovery of DP / DR:

I) Initial state of consciousness depersonalized and derealized: Over the years you learn to live with just the left hemisphere input, **emotions are simulated, you learn to ignore and manage the annoying situations** (avoiding crowds, view of landscapes and open spaces, and many other things ...) **and can live without thinking much about it**. BUT YOU ARE ALWAYS AWARE THAT YOU ARE NOT WELL YET. Periodically the DP / DR will occupy your mind and you might try again to find a solution, probably unsuccessfully. When daily life, your work or your studies demand your attention then you will forget the issue for once and will continue living on your own.

II) Phase of conscious exercises: We can start with exercise number 1 half an hour every afternoon and consciously face the objects and examine our moving body. We often will become frustrated and return home with apparently no improvement at all. But if you remain doing efforts based on (1) **asking for the brain that performs functions that are only known by the right hemisphere** and (2) **remembering how you lived when you were alright** we will open a minimum neuronal path to the sensory and emotional information stored there.

WHAT YOU HAVE TO DO IS PRECISELY THE ACTIVITIES THAT INCREASE THE DP/DR FEELING. WHEN WE ARE MORE CONSCIOUS THAT WE ARE IMPOTENT TO FULFILL THEM. SO THEY MAY INCREASE YOUR LEVEL OF ANXIETY. => That's why these exercises" cannot be take us more than 1/2 hour at first, until we get to Phase III.

This phase is critical. It is when we will be tempted to give up. Again resignation. We still will be well, perhaps not yet feel almost emotions but notice that **something is going well**. We will be **forcing** the right hemisphere to work. "i.e. *evoking images and objects from the past and retrieving memories associated with color shades we perceive* ".

Don't GET OBSESSED WITH THE RECOVERY; IT IS A TIME TO RELAX, TO HAVE A WALK... USING YOUR SENSES, TRYING TO DO THE EXERCISES AND HAVING FUN. YOU DON'T HAVE ANYTHING TO LOSE!

During this phase we will alternate outdoor exercises with others that can be done at home. This phase may be long, in my case from six months to a year.

III) Initial phase of normality

There will come a day when, by repeating the exercises, surprisingly, we can do them even outside the half an hour and with not too much difficulty. We will return to normalcy, improve our vision, our memory will be reinforced, time perception will return to normality, our memory, our tastes and preferences and the most important thing, we will be able to access the **emotions** . WE WILL BE **A COMPLETE PERSON AGAIN AND FINALLY WE WILL BREATH AND FIND INNER PEACE.**

7.5   WHEN WILL I KNOW THAT I AM CURED?

- Because now **I enjoy open landscapes**.
- Because I'm going to crowded **shopping malls** plenty of different objects and I do not feel "overwhelmed" in these situations.
- Because **I distinguish between countless shades of different colors** .
- Because **I can hear all** the sounds **closest** and relate them to others I've heard in the past.
- Because going through the section **of perfumes** of a mall is a **parade of exciting smells**

- Because while I am driving I can to be unfocused a little off the road and **enjoy everything I see around,** look at the drivers of other cars, ...

- Because I utter **words that show emotion** naturally. I can kiss and hug my children with total feeling of what I'm doing. I mean consciously.
- Because I can easily access **what I did yesterday and the day before yesterday**, or last week.

- Because now I know **what is falling in love again with my wife**.
- Because **when I look at the clock I can see it as something natural** and does not overflow me. **The time of the day guides me**.
- Because now I'm **spontaneous** and I can jump to touch the leaves of the trees or to kick a can to score a goal between two cars, I can phone a friend spontaneously whenever I want...
- For **so many reasons** ...

NEVER GIVE UP SEARCHING A SOLUTION TO YOUR DP / DR!

Even if you're used to it

DON'T WASTE YOUR LIFE ANYMORE WITHIN THAT CELL

I know what you have to do

santos.barrioscanseco@gmail.com

8 CONCLUSIONS

That ends this **first volume** about Depersonalization and Derealization being aware that there are many things missing. I have many more aspects to provide but time is limited and the lives of patients affected by DPDR are wasting while I am writing these final lines. This is why I don't want to delay more the publication of the written so far since I believe it could be very useful **to spread the name of this disorder** and gather as soon as possible the basic exercises of this treatment **at a single place**.

I have avoided from copy & paste existing documentation from others books or simply from collect patient testimonials affected by this disorder. I think there are enough testimonials on Facebook groups as somebody could perceive the full scale of the problem we are facing. *Jeffrey Abugel* well pointed out in his book "*Stranger to my self*" that DPDR is becoming a **silent epidemic** threatening a growing number of people around the world.

My theory about the nature of the DPDR as a partial disconnection or weakening between both brain hemispheres and/or limbic system should be investigated rigorously with a set of test subjects in order to check its validity. I strongly believe, because I lived it from the inside, that **the different disturbing sensations from depersonalization and derealization are caused by this lack of synchronization between hemispheres**, but I understand this **is not enough for the scientific and medical communities**.

It's missing a chapter about the current **pharmacological treatments** which are being prescribed to those patients affected by DPDR in psychiatric consultations. According to all the testimonials from patients medication doesn't seem to solve completely the problem although it can alleviate the symptoms enough to live a semi-normal life. A number of them are at the crossroad of what to do with the medication, Must I continue or must I stop taking it? And if I continue taking them the question is: for how long? Must I take them forever?

Another missing subject is talking about DPDR prevention. It is widely known that prevention is better than cure and specially respect to DPDR disorder.

Typically **this disorder is considered as chronic by medical professionals**, it is supposed sometime it will disappear by itself (or not!) and patient probably will have to accustom himself to live forever together with those strange sensations.

I firmly believe that knowing the nature of this syndrome the patient can slowly deal with the huge task of reconnecting the lost, atrophied, disturbed connections by the powerful psycho-neurological effect of the generalized anxiety. There is a critical moment when **anxiety stops growing and a great blackout happened, the neurochemical change which produces brain enters in a disconnection of reality mode** in order to defend itself from unbearable emotions. From that moment on the problem is not strictly psychological but in certain way neurological as well.

Recovery shouldn't be left to chance because if my hypothesis are correct there are still many exercises to do which could help the patient to head for the right direction and feel again a unique human being with its own personality. **Only a conscious and active effort by the individual is suitable for fully solving the problem.** Trusting in meds or simply letting the time passes passively it's useless.

The apathetic, powerless and no-motivated character, the intrusive thoughts, the spatial-temporal confusion or even the difficulty on reading texts caused by DPDR could make on many occasions patients **cannot do the proposed exercises of this book** with sufficient consistency to escape from this condition. DPDR may cause affected patients feel chained within a timeless routine which locks them up and makes their situation lasts for undefined time, as letting their selves go and simply don't fix the dissociation because it is an **stable brain state**.

They let the time pass by, procrastinating and delaying their problem without one single measure being taken against it. So, I also believe it's **necessary to receive local support by means of trained therapists** who physically accompany patients when walking. They also might encourage and guide them through a correct practice of Santos Barrios' exercises.

I sincerely hope this book let accomplish the main proposed objectives, basically spreading throughout the world the existence of this dissociation and that a growing number of people affected by dpdr can improve the quality of their lives recovering step by step. **Nobody deserves to live without a direction, without a SELF.**

Those who cannot handle this state despite all efforts, time and treatments please **contact me** (santos.barrioscanseco@gmail.com) or with the association ASEDEP (asedep@outlook.es) in order to set an appointment, physical or virtual and assess the possibility of start a support and accompaniment action within your recovery process.

I also **invite all the psychology/psychiatry professionals who want to deepen within this disorder to contact me** to review more concrete details and in that way advance in the setting of a definitive treatment against this set of so disturbing symptoms.

March, 2017

Santos Barrios Canseco

President of the People Affected by Depersonalization and Derealization Spanish Association (ASEDEP)

santos.barrioscanseco@gmail.com

NOTE: Before sending this book to the printer's or uploading to the cloud through Internet I would like to address those persons, many of them friends as well, who are still suffering quietly this disorder.

I know many of you have **lost hope** to recover your personality and that you have resigned yourself to wander around life acting, dissimulating normalcy with family, workmates or friends. Many of you are even **afraid of returning to be the same person** previous to the depersonalization or derealization disorder, since any trauma or memory which harmed you is still there, waiting for you. Others are **afraid of never being ok**, not being able to remove the habit of self-examination searching for the DPDR symptoms, wondering who are you, afraid of never being able to look your image in the mirror without raising existential questions.

Others of you are afraid of not being able to recognize the day of your recovery and let that moment passes away.

Others think **once broken by DPDR, there is no way to put back your pieces together again**. Maybe thinking you have lost the innocence about the reality of the world and about your SELF. Maybe thinking the recurrent and philosophical thoughts which fill your mind are forever and never will disappear.

Others maybe think it's not so bad living dissociated, or even see the positive side. A way of self-convincing it's not necessary to treat this disorder anymore.

Many of you even **tired of being tired** about thinking about this THING.

I understand all your fears and worries but my message is clear and strong:

Yes, we can and we must try to abandon this state!!

APPENDIX

TEMPLATE FOR "THE STORY OF MY LIFE" EXERCISE

Age												
	JAN	FEB	MAR	APR	MAY	JUN	JUL	AUG	SEP	OCT	NOV	DEC
Year												

DECALOGUE TO FOLLOW

1. I will devote **just half an hour a day** to my recovery process **in solitude.**
2. I will **avoid stressful situations.** I'll try **not being in a hurry** anymore.
3. I will **often notice where my body** parts are, my clothes and my position in space.
4. I will **stop of wondering philosophical questions** and feel more with my senses.
5. I **won't focus** long time in any mental/abstract activity, doing frequent reconnections with reality (place, body, things, time and emotions) seeing actively in 3D.
6. I **will go back in time (regression)** to feel like the way I used to when I was OK.
7. I **will compare the place I am** with other similar places from my past.
8. I will ask **when were the first time in my life** I saw that object, I was at that place, I heard that sound...
9. I will **pay attention to the people surrounding** me wondering what they are probably thinking of me.
10. I will **take my family and close friends' opinion into account** to recover lost habits and **references.**

DPDR AUTODIAGNOSTIC TEST

(Ask for the .xls and send the filled form to santos.barrioscanseco@gmail.com)

DEPERSONALIZATION/DEREALIZATION DIAGNOSTIC TEST v1.0
(c) Santos Barrios

SYMPTOM FREQUENCY (fill in with a X where appropriate)

Nº	Name	Description of the symptom	Never	Sometimes	Often	Always
1	Unreality	Do you have the feeling the world is unreal, do you perceive it as a dream?				
2	Self-examination	Do you feel as an observer of your own body? Your body moves and you don't control it completely.				
3	Lack of motivation and goals in life	Have you lost interest in most of the activities? Nothing can excite you				
4	Preferences and joy lost	Have you missed the pleasure for doing things that previously pleased you?, Do you notice nothing makes you glad?, Are you unable to be happy?				
5	Uncontrolled rational thoughts	Do you usually wonder the because of the things?, Do you need to understand how everything works?, Do you think life is not worth living?				
6	Altered perception of passing of time	Is it hard for you feeling how the time goes by?, Do you feel disgusted when you look at the time on a clock?, While you are focused on something... don't you know when to stop?				
7	Depersonalization	Do you feel as nobody? As if you doubt you have lived a life previously to suffer this disorder.				
8	Tendency to defocus your gaze	Do you usually let your gaze be defocused / lost?				
9	Inhability to feel emotions	In a given situation you know you should feel an emotion (sadness, happiness, ...)... are you feeling nothing?				
10	Strangeness of your own body	When looking your hands you feel them as rare, strange, as if they don't belong completely to you?				
11	Flat vision	Do you see everything flatter, less deeper than before?				
12	Worse memory than before	Is it hard for you to remember certain things that you previously used to remember effortless?				
13	Spatial disorientation	Out of home are you afraid of get lost, as if you didn't know how to orient properly?				
14	Incomprehension of the others	Do you usually perceive the rest of human beings as strange, as puppets or cartoons? As if you could not understand their existence.				
15	Grayer/darker vision	Is the world more gray now, feeling that colours don't mean anything for you?				
16	Strangeness of your own image	When you look your own face at the mirror or at a picture do you feel uncomfortable and strangeness, as if you could not identify with that person that is watching?				
17	Macropsia/Micropsia	Sometimes you cannot perceive adequately the size of the objects, even parts of your body.				
18	Slow and burdensome vision	Is it hard for you observing things, as if your eyes were lazier than normal?, Do you think your gaze is slower than before?				
19	Difficulty for planning	Does it takes much effort to plan what you are going to do within a specific time period, as an afternoon, a couple of hours,...?				
20	Strangeness of your own voice	Do you feel that your voice sounds strange, as it wasn't yours completely?				
21	Strange sounds	Are you uncomfortable listening to usual sounds coming from the street or inside your house?, do they seem strange although you know they shouldn't because you have heard them in the past?				
22	Irrelevant position of the body	Do you use to look at the position of your feet, hands and the rest of your body?				
23	Lack of attention to physical aspect	Have you stopped worrying about the style, colour or shape of the clothes you wear?, Is your aspect not important any more?, Have you stopped showing off before others?				
24	Agoraphobia	Do you feel uncomfortable when you go out in the street?, Are you overwhelmed in open air areas?				
25	Automatic actions	Are you surprised acting robotically, in automatic way?				
26	Out of place within human groups	When you meet a group of friends do you feel you don't know how to behave adequately, whom listen to?, Do you feel lost and disconnected from the group?				
27	Sleepiness. Lack of energy	Do you usually feel more tired than before and with the desire to rest?				
28	Ingravity - not feeling your own weight	When walking on the street, do you feel weightless?				
29	Decision making - procrastination	Do you usually tend to delay decision making? Is it hard to come to a decision?				
30	Difficulty to pay attention	Is it hard for you to pay attention and your thoughts easily mislead you? Can you keep a conversation without difficulty?				
31	Overwhelming sensation	Do you usually feel your brain is fed up, overloaded with repetitive thoughts?				
32	Solipsism	Do you think that all that exists probably is a fiction invented by your mind?				
33	Inhability to evoke past situations	Do you note it is hard for you evoking what you've just lived through? that once you live an experience it is difficult for you to remember it				
34	Insecurity	Have you stopped doing things because you feel you won't be able to do them? Do you note unsecurity about your self?				
35	Uncomfortable inside malls or crowds	Do you feel overwhelmed when you enter a large, crowded, and plenty of stimuli shopping center? Do you use to have a bad time in them?				
36	Difficult reading	Since suffering this disorder, is it harder for you to retain what you read?, Has your concentration level dropped? Don't you enjoy reading anymore?				
37	Numb senses - Detachment from the world	Do you feel detached from the world, as separated by an invisible veil that does not let you perceive everything directly?				
38	Blurry vision	Is it hard to observe things because you perceive like a fog, something that prevents you to see clearly? Do you take longer than usual to find objects?				
39	Tunnel vision	When walking or driving a car, do you find it hard to take your eyes off the front to observe other people left and right?				
40	Awakening from the scratch	As soon as you get awake on the bed, do you feel there is no reason to get up?, Don't you know when to do it, as if you should start from the scratch everyday?				

February 2016 - (c) Santos Barrios Canseco

BLOG, VIDEOS and ASEDEP ASSOCIATION

This first volume represents one of the first books written by a Spanish author about Depersonalization and Derealization Disorder. It is based on different posts I published simultaneously in both languages, Spanish and English:

      http://dpdrspain.blogspot.com,   in Spanish

      http://dpdrenglish.blogspot.com,   In English

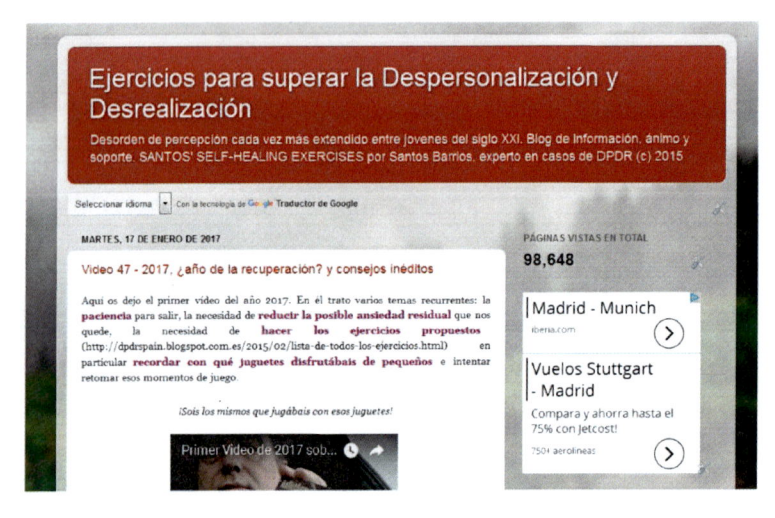

In these two blogs there is and there will be additional information about DPDR non-existing inside the books and vice versa. One of the main benefits of this book is serving as a reference manual where **the first 20 exercises of my natural method** to escape from DPDR state **can be found**.

Also on **YouTube** (CANAL DPDR, Spanish language) you can access to videos recorded as a support to understand better the nature of the exercises and give relief to all the people suffering this disturbing syndrome daily. The first Spanish association, ASEDEP, is already present in Facebook and it has more than fifty members in 2018.

      http://www.facebook.com/ASEDEP